It is my distinct honor to recomme ᴜ ᴜᴏᴏᴋ ᴊᴏᴜ*Holes*. Her revelation on the soul, received through her intimate relationship with the Father, is transformational and will enlighten and bring deep healing to many. Through this teaching, she not only imparts spiritual knowledge, but her own soul, just as the apostle Paul did to the church at Thessalonica (see 1 Thessalonians 2:8). I see many traumas being instantly healed through reading *Soul Holes*! Get ready to be transformed!

Myles Kilby
Myles Kilby Ministries
Brunswick, Georgia

This book on *Soul Holes* is a profound revelation and insight the Body of Christ desperately needs. Rebecca is genuinely gifted in explaining the deep things of God in a way that is easy to comprehend and leaves you with a hunger for more. It's a practical teaching that will challenge you to think outside the box and examine yourself. As you read, repent, and apply the teaching to your life, you will be changed for the better.

Greg and Kymberly Lowery
Pastors, Soperton Church of God

The God that we see in this book of *Soul Holes* also said:

> *Dear friends, now we are children of God, and what we will have*
> *not yet been made known. But we know that when Christ appears,*
> *we shall be like him, for we shall see him as he is.*   1 John 3:2

The God who appears to you is the God who you begin to reflect to other people. Rebecca walks in His glory for His Kingdom. We need to see God for who He is. Once you fill those soul holes in your life, things begin to line up with our King Jesus. But if you're not prepared spiritually and have your soul holes filled, you won't be ready to receive the blessings of the Lord! You could miss out on the very things you are hoping for. Extraordinary moments are coming, and great moments will astound you.

Glory! Jesus is King!
Johnny & Kim Grenade
J & K Creations

As Rebecca King writes in *Soul Holes,* "God is looking for somewhere to rest His glory." She is someone upon whom God has rested His glory. Like a rainbow across her face, God shines through her, and this book is a manifestation of that divine shining.

Eric Gilmour
Sonship International

It is with great pleasure that I write an endorsement for Rebecca King's new work on healing the holes in your soul. I have both witnessed the transformation in her own life and the positive influence she has on others around her through her own personal experience. Rebecca's insight into how we can recover from unhealed soul wounds comes from great personal insight, experience, and transformation. When many of us are cheated out of happy childhoods, loving relationships, the wonder of motherhood, or even from good health, we begin to blame others. Often, the people who are close to us pay the greatest price for our traumatic experience. Sometimes we even blame God. Rebecca explains how we set ourselves up for a lifetime of disappointment when we create rules and expectations for others to live by. The questions she asks is: "Have you let your anger and disappointment fester into bitterness that is now eating a hole in your soul? Will you let the past define your future? Will you continue to fill that wound with wrong choices?" Rebecca masters the definition of finding true peace and healing as she points the way through the path of unconditional love and forgiveness.

David L. Ramer
Pastor, Glory Fire Church
Lake Mary, Florida

SOUL HOLES

McDougal & Associates
Servants of Christ and Stewards of the
Mysteries of God

6/2/05

To JOSHUA
AND GANG,
I love you guys.

Rebunah King

To God Be All the
Glory... glory

SOUL HOLES

AND HOW THEY CAN BE HEALED

REBECCA L. KING

Published by:

McDougal & Associates
18896 Greenwell Springs Road
Greenwell Springs, LA 70739

www.ThePublishedWord.com

McDougal & Associates is dedicated to spreading the Gospel of the Lord Jesus Christ to as many people as possible in the shortest time possible.

ISBN: 978-1-950398-55-3

Printed on demand in the U.S., the U.K., Australia and the U.A.E.
For Worldwide Distribution

DEDICATION

I would like to dedicate this book to the greatest woman in my life. The fact that I lived inside of you for the first nine months of my establishment created a bond between us that can never be severed. I loved you the first time my heart beat inside of yours. Your eyes comforted me, your voice guided me, and your love sustained me. You are a beautiful person, and I am blessed to call you Mom.

CORENE MARIE HANCOCK KING

ACKNOWLEDGMENTS

I would like to acknowledge all those who helped make this book a reality:

- My editors: *Brenda Aultman, Liz Thomas* and *Harold McDougal,* for making my text say what it needed to say.

- The artist: *Erin Allison,* for taking the original cover concept God gave me and perfecting it.

- The illustrator: *Miranda Cargle,* for her lovely illustrations.

I would also like to acknowledge:

- All those who encouraged me along this journey.

- *Glory Fire Congregation,* for probing me to scribe the pages of this God-given guide.

DISCLAIMER

Rebecca King Ministries LLC does not seek to be in conflict with any church denomination, organized religion, medical or psychiatric practice. It is not to be compared to or conflicted with any other religious beliefs, doctrines, or practices. It is not part of medicine or psychology, but rather an awareness of understanding the body and mind as they relate to God. It is about the belief that behind every natural effect there lies an underlying spiritual cause. It is a belief that what our minds conceive our bodies are able to achieve.

This information is intended for those who know that in the spirit more insights are revealed than in the natural. This information is to inform you of spiritual matters that can greatly improve the health of your body. These insights are intended to help you find the answers you have been searching for and to encourage you while in the process. This information is not a substitute for any medication, medical advice, or prescribed treatment therapy. It is not to disagree with a doctor's diagnosis, but rather to show you that there is often more involved than a doctor's eyes can see. It is a belief that what you discuss with your physician is to be honored and considered to be a confirmation of your present affliction.

At no point is it a belief that you should stop taking prescribed medications, treatments, and/or therapy, and it is highly advised that you always seek the counsel of medical professionals. Rebecca King Ministries and/or Rebecca L. King are not responsible for any person's disease or for the healing of others. However, they can share with people what they have seen that has help them overcome traumas and dilemmas that distort the truth. This information could be the cause of inflammation of the soul, which could cause inflammation of the body.

Rebecca does what the Holy Spirit instructs and leaves it all in the hands of her Heavenly Father. She administers the Holy Scriptures of God's Word and relies confidently on His Holy Spirit to instruct and advise.

There is no guarantee that any person will be healed or any disease will be prevented. The fruits of this teaching will come forth out of the relationship formed between the person and God based on insights shared at the time of ministry. Rebecca King Ministries LLC is patterned after the healing scriptures:

> *But he was wounded for our transgressions, he was bruised for our iniquities: the chastisement of our peace was upon him; and with his stripes we are healed.* **Isaiah 53:5**

> *Beloved, I wish above all things that thou mayest prosper and be in health, even as thy soul prospereth.* **3 John 2**

> *And these signs shall follow them that believe; In my name shall they cast out devils; they shall speak with new tongues; they shall take up serpents; and if they drink any deadly thing, it shall not hurt them; they shall lay hands on the sick, and they shall recover.* **Mark 16:17-18**

> *But when Jesus heard it, he answered him, saying, Fear not: believe only, and she shall be made whole.* **Luke 8:50**

I pray that Rebecca King Ministries LLC, by way of the Holy Scriptures of God, relationship, and intimacy, will be able to help you overcome afflictions that have plagued the Body of Christ.

CONTENTS

Foreword by Joshua Mills 13

About the Cover... 14

A Letter from the Author 17

1. What Is a Soul Hole? 19

2. Be Ye Holy, Not Holey 55

3. Identifying Your Soul Holes......................... 83

4. A Three-Fold Chord 111

5. Denying and Dying 143

6. Name It, but Don't blame It 167

7. Free Indeed 191

Author Contact Page 214

FOREWORD BY JOSHUA MILLS

My fellow minister and dear friend, Rebecca King, walks in the Spirit of revelation. This is the way she operates in ministry, and in this same flow, she also writes her books that bring fresh insight and understanding to the Body of Christ. This latest book, *Soul Holes*, offers us all a glimpse into the world of soul-healing—how to attain it, walk in it, and prosper in such a way that it overflows into a physical manifestation of healing, spiritual strength, and ultimate success in every area of our lives.

I'm thankful that Rebecca has taken the time to research the Scriptures, write from personal experience, and deliver to us this much-needed revelation. Every person you know should have a copy of this book on hand. Get one for yourself and a few more copies for those you love. It's time for spiritual, emotional, and physical wounds to be healed, as you learn how to live in the freedom of the Spirit!

Joshua Mills
International Glory Ministries
Bestselling author, Power Portals *&* Creative Glory
www.joshuamills.com

ABOUT THE COVER

As I celebrate my twenty-fifth year of sobriety, I am led to reflect upon the signs that directed me to my current path. Life can bring jolts of uncertainty that develop you into the person God desired you to become. He doesn't allow bad things to happen to good people; He allows good people to endure bad things.

Carefree, curious, and contagious, I thought life was good. What could be better than having a good time? However, all good times that are not righteous come to an end. My best friend and I were self-medicating for entertainment and conquering our porous conditions, when I needed to be excused from the semi-unconscious lifestyle to attend to the affairs of my soul.

Invitation after invitation, I turned down the opportunity to continue upon that destructive pathway. My intuition was strong and what appeared to be a craft of some sort turned into a design of destiny. A mere black stick man painted upon a white canvas of carefulness became the focus of my attention. My mornings, afternoons and nights were consumed with the passion for perfection, as my brush stroked each fabric angle.

Somehow my soul knew the importance of my containment. However, my best friend felt the emotions of betrayal, rejection, and abandonment as I steadfastly locked into this mysterious outline of mine.

Once I finished the design, a small voice told me to create another canvas with the opposite colors. I began to draw another sick man (white this time) with a black background. This project took weeks to complete. Meanwhile, my best friend continued on the road of self-abandonment.

Early one morning I awakened from a nightmare. I was underwater and couldn't breathe. I rushed to the top of the water, and suddenly emerged and gasped for air. When I woke up, I was sitting up in the bed in a cold sweat.

Several hours later, I was awakened again by a knock on the door. It was my mother. She was frantic and asked me to dress quickly and get in the car. I knew it wasn't good by the look on her face. My nightmare was now my reality. My friend was gone. On a cold Christmas Eve morning, she was no longer. Her soul had vanished like a vapor of smoke.

As I visited the wreck site and looked within the twisted metal of the vehicle, I saw a Christmas card covered with blood. It was addressed to me, and it said, "I hope you have the best Christmas ever." Little did I know that the two paintings that had captured the essence of my being would keep me from accompanying my friend as she succumbed to premature death. It wasn't the paintings that saved me; it was my choice to deny what I wanted over the voice I heard inside my soul. That is the meaning of the cover so wonderfully captured by Erin Allison.

15

YE HAVE SOWN MUCH, AND BRING IN LITTLE;
YE EAT, BUT YE HAVE NOT ENOUGH;
YE DRINK, BUT YE ARE NOT FILLED WITH DRINK;
YE CLOTHE YOU, BUT THERE IS NONE WARM;
AND HE THAT EARNETH WAGES
EARNETH WAGES TO PUT IT INTO
A BAG WITH HOLES.
— HAGGAI 1:6

A Letter from the Author

Many times we fall short of God's glory because of the lack of knowledge concerning our own souls. Our soul has the ability to overcome all things, yet our soul can also be overcome. We must be careful not to assume that our soul is only related to salvation. The soul is the part of your being that is responsible for making decisions. I minister to many people who never consider the ramifications of the decisions they have allowed their souls to make. One poor decision in the soul can bring dysfunction to one's body in the future.

I minister to a lot of physically, mentally, and emotionally sick people. By the time the people call me for ministry, they are desperate because their affliction is overriding their soul. It takes time for me to lead them back to the original entry point of their affliction. In other words, the lack of knowledge concerning the soul brings many afflictions to the physical body. In order to be set free in the body, we must first be set free in the soul.

In this book, we will define each human aspect of our individuality and also every component of our soul. We will learn how to take responsibility for each aspect and categorize each component of the soul, depending on the amount of damage that has been done. Past pains, traumas, and negative emotions have played a role in the condition of our wellbeing. As we receive this God-given insight, we can then understand how to cooperate with our current condition and allow the truth of God to set us free. Once responsibility is taken and the truth is applied, we can finally walk in the signs, wonders, and miracles of God ourselves.

Come with me on this journey, to find peace for your mind, rest for your soul, and healing for your body.

Rebecca L. King
Nashville, Georgia

CHAPTER 1

WHAT IS A SOUL HOLE?

Jesus said unto him, Thou shalt love the Lord thy God with all thy heart, and with all thy soul, and with all thy mind.   Matthew 22:37

What is a soul hole? A soul hole is an interruption in your soul that leaves an indention of emotional issues. This emotional indention will affect the future health of your emotions and relationships. An indention is created by extreme negative emotions, traumas, painful experiences, and/or invalidations. Soul holes are places of confusion, emptiness, or deficiency within the mind, the will, the emotions, the imagination, or the memory.

Most soul holes are formed out of abuse, neglect, and lack of knowledge. Many of our soul holes are formed from stuffing our emotions when we don't know how to deal with the pain involved. Many soul holes can stem from a disturbed childhood. When soul holes are not filled, they have the potential, through time, to grow deeper and wider. Soul holes never just fade away. They must be dealt with in order to be filled and healed. Soul holes can be passed down as misinformation to future generations.

Soul holes are the evidence of serious deficiencies within the inner man that must be addressed as compliable[1] issues in order for a person to be made whole. Undealt-with issues within a soul will eventually cause afflictions in the physical body. An undealt-with issue in one's soul results from not knowing how to deal with the issue at hand, thus causing one's soul to close. Soul holes that are not dealt with have the ability to affect you in many ways: mentally, physically, emotionally, spiritually, relationally, and financially.

Yes, poverty is due to soul holes! The soul goal is to love the Lord and others out of our wholeness. But, in order to do so, we must get our soul holes healed and filled. How can we accomplish this when our soul has been so full of holes? I am reminded of a passage of scripture that describes soul holes perfectly:

> *Ye have sown much, and bring in little; ye eat, but ye have not enough; ye drink, but ye are not filled with drink; ye clothe you, but there is none warm; and he that earneth wages earneth wages to put it into a bag with holes.* Haggai 1:6

The soul is where we make all our decisions. Every person is assigned a soul. Regardless of certain beliefs, no one shares a uni-soul with another human being. The dictionary defines <u>soul</u> as "the immaterial essence of a living being." The soul

1. To me "compliable" means the issues I must agree with in order to come out of agreement with the enemy of my soul.

is the part of you that makes you who you are. Fortunately, the soul only makes up one-third of your humanistic totality, but it has the ability to overcome the other two-thirds of your mortal makeup. The other two aspects are the spirit and the body. It takes all three of these to make a human being whole. God desires to wholly sanctify His people, in spirit, body, and soul:

> *And the very God of peace sanctify you wholly; and I pray God your whole spirit and soul and body be preserved blameless unto the coming of our Lord Jesus Christ.* 1 Thessalonians 5:23

God desires to make us whole. Soul holes have the ability to interrupt completeness and unity. All three aspects of humanity need to be analyzed—three-in-one, and individually. We will analyze the soul first, recognizing it as the deciding factor of humanity.

THE COMPONENTS OF THE SOUL

There are five components of the soul: the mind, the will, the emotions, the imagination, and the memory. The *mind* (which includes thought processes, experiences, feelings, consciousness, and intellect) is the part of a person that enables him or her to be aware of the world. The *will* is the capability to make conscious choices, decisions, intentions, and actions that follow mental thoughts. *Emotions* are the evidence of the natural instinctive state of the mind caused by situations and relations. The *imagination* is the part of our

21

soul that forms new ideas and/or concepts concerning the unknown. The *memory* makes up the storage compartment of our soul, enabling us to store information and reproduce or recall what has been learned. Some people call the memory "a bank" because it is a place for you to store your valuable memories.

Now that we have considered the five components of the soul, let us move on to a discussion of the other two aspects.

WHAT IS THE SPIRIT OF A MAN?

The *spirit* of a man is the part of mankind that has been with God since before the foundation of the world:

> *Before I formed thee in the belly I knew thee; and before thou camest forth out of the womb I sanctified thee, and I ordained thee a prophet unto the nations.*
>
> Jeremiah 1:5

After a person's death, their spirit is the part of them that returns back from whence it came:

> *Then shall the dust return to the earth as it was: and the spirit shall return unto God who gave it.*
>
> Ecclesiastes 12:7

The spirit of a man also includes intellect, emotions, fears, passion, and creativity. In comparison, the spirit somewhat mirrors the soul, but it is the soul of a man that determines the final outcome. The soul is where the will lies.

Soul holes have the ability to cause untruths to seem true. The *will* of a person is what determines his or her destiny. The spirit has the ability to see the truth of God without the effects of emotional damage. Unfortunately, once the soul has been extremely interrupted, it has the ability to influence the spirit. Have you ever heard the statement, *"Don't break a child's spirit?"* Our spirit can be broken by other people and also by our own soul. If one's spirit is broken, the only way to healing is to offer that broken spirit to God:

> *The sacrifices of God are a broken spirit: a bro-*
> *ken and contrite heart, O God, thou wilt not*
> *despise.* Psalm 51:17

Our spirit has the potential to be the strongest aspect because it was with God before the foundation of the world. It is the soul that has the power to choose. Therefore, your soul usually overrides your spirit. Basically, whichever aspect you feed the most will tend to be the strongest.

WHICHEVER ASPECT YOU FEED THE MOST WILL BECOME THE STRONGEST!

Before God breathed the breath of life into our nostrils and we became living souls, our spirits were with God:

So God created man in his own image, in the image of God created he him; male and female created he them.   Genesis 1:27

In other words, our spirit was with God before He created our soul to be housed in our body of clay:

What? know ye not that your body is the temple of the Holy Ghost which is in you, which ye have of God, and ye are not your own?   1 Corinthians 6:19

Have you ever met a person and felt like you have known them for years? It is because you have. God created all our spirits simultaneously because there was no "time" before the foundation of the world. When someone says to me, "I know you from somewhere," and I have never met them before, I know that their spirit is bearing witness with my spirit:

The Spirit itself beareth witness with our spirit, that we are the children of God.   Romans 8:16

God is no respecter of persons:

Then Peter opened his mouth, and said, Of a truth I perceive that God is no respecter of persons.   Acts 10:34

When God created our spirits, He created us all at once. This was in the deep!

CONSIDERING THE BODY

The next aspect of the human existence is the *body*. The body is the physical structure which includes the bones, the flesh, and the organs. The body actually houses the soul and spirit and completes the human being. The physical body is influenced greatly by both the spirit and the soul. As a matter of fact, the body manifests an outward appearance of the inner man:

> *A good man out of the good treasure of his heart bringeth forth that which is good; and an evil man out of the evil treasure of his heart bringeth forth that which is evil: for of the abundance of the heart his mouth speaketh.*　　　Luke 6:45

The body takes on the appearance of what is going on in both the spirit and the soul. The body is the truth teller of the spirit and soul. You can hide issues in your soul, but you cannot hide issues in your body.

Anatomically, the body is, by far, the most amazing structure in the world. At birth, our spirit came into our body, and our soul became alive:

> *And the LORD God formed man of the dust of the ground, and breathed into his nostrils the breath of life; and man became a living soul.*　　Genesis 2:7

25

An interesting fact about the body is that it has the ability to heal itself. Once the soul and spirit come into agreement with the truth, the source of identity deficiency can be revealed, and the truth sets you free so that you can be made whole.

You were once all spirit (before the Fall). Then deception brought forth the conception of your natural being. Therefore, conception holds the deception and has need of the truth to set us free. This may not mean anything to you, if you haven't been seeking the truth, but if you have been seeking truth, this will make total sense. Anything other than the truth is a deficiency.

Soul holes are intended to indent your identity and steal God's charismatic creation. In other words, if you are not secure in who God made you to be, chances are you have soul holes that disable you and prevent from being made whole. In this case, identity deficiencies are soul holes that weaken the body, thus keeping it from containing the substance of God's presence, which is truth.

Since the soul is the aspect that makes choices, if it is weakened by soul holes, it cannot contain the presence of God. If the soul was a bucket that had holes, it could not contain water. Soul holes weaken the true eternal identity that we are supposed to display while on the earth. The spirit in us has been with God, yet it is influenced by the weakened soul. And the body can only contain what the soul interprets. Therefore, if the soul has holes, the body perceives it as an interruption because its interpretation stems from deception instead of truth.

Soul holes are identity and intimacy robbers. The purpose of the bucket (soul) is to hold the water that will saturate the whole body. This explains why so many Christians are dry. Have you ever wondered why your skin gets dry? It is because you were made from dust! The only way to get free from dryness is to be saturated by the presence of God. Fortunately, your past soul holes, once filled with God's glory, have the ability to soak up God's presence like a sponge.

> **SOUL HOLES ARE IDENTITY AND INTIMACY ROBBERS!**

Wholeness is our true identity, and anything less than wholeness makes us question who we are. In other words, when we identify the holes in our soul and when we come out of agreement with the lies and repent, then our bodies can be saturated with healing. Again, we must identify the soul holes, come out of agreement and denial, repent and ask God to allow His glory to fill our soul holes.

May I lead you in a prayer?

Dear Heavenly Father,

I purpose and choose with my free will to repent for any and all fear, rejection, and abandonment that I have harbored in my heart as sin. Lord, I ask You to forgive me, and I forgive myself for any ways I have allowed these issues to indent my soul. I forgive all others for the ways in which they have hurt me. I come out of agreement with my soul holes now, in Jesus' name.

Lord, fill me with Your glory and set me free. Holy Spirit, please speak your words of truth.

Amen!

DOES GOD HAVE A SOUL?

First, we must discuss the foundation of our spirit, soul, and body. Many times I will ask my audience, "Does God have a soul?" I find this interesting because about half the people know the truth. Yes, God has a soul, or we could not have one:

> *And I set my tabernacle among you: and my soul shall not abhor you.* Leviticus 26:11

The only difference in God's soul and man's soul is *sin*. Man's soul is contaminated with sin, but God's soul has never been tainted.

The soul is the most misunderstood aspect of the human body. If the enemy wants my soul so badly, it must be worth something. Yes, the soul is the value of a human being.

Interestingly enough, my studies of the inner soul lead me to the importance of understanding the trinity of God. The trinity of God brings us into the totality of the soul, making it possible for us to understand the depths of our beings. Having three aspects makes us dimensional. If you do not understand dimensional, you may not be intentional. We must come into the understanding that God has given us the gift of His Triune to help us understand the spirit, body, and soul.

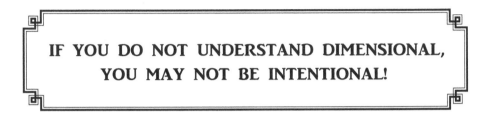

IF YOU DO NOT UNDERSTAND DIMENSIONAL, YOU MAY NOT BE INTENTIONAL!

The word *trinity* means "the state of being three." When we understand the importance of the three, then we can truly be free. Humanly, this is how all three aspects can operate together. If one of the three gets damaged, it has the potential to greatly affect the other two. Not so with God. His triune is flawless in itself.

As humans, we are flawed because of sin. Therefore, each of us has to work out his or her own salvation:

> *Wherefore, my beloved, as ye have always obeyed, not as in my presence only, but now much more in my absence, work out your own salvation with fear and trembling.* Philippians 2:12

EXAMINING THE TRINITY OF GOD

God the Father, God the Son, and God the Holy Spirit make up the trinity of God. Although this word, *trinity*, is not found in the Bible, it well describes the three-in-one capabilities of God. We clearly see in the Scriptures that the trinity works as the totality of eternity. It is the completion of the Godhead, and it is demonstrated here on earth as it is in heaven.

The triangle is the most accurate angle measurement to illustrate how the Trinity operates:

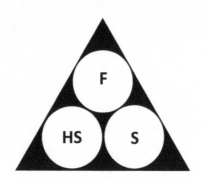

This is where wholeness comes in:

And the very God of peace sanctify you wholly; and I pray God your whole spirit and soul and body be

preserved blameless unto the coming of our Lord Jesus
Christ.   1 Thessalonians 5:23

We were created in God's image. Therefore, everything that He is He created us to be. If He has a soul, then He gave us a soul:

Behold my servant, whom I have chosen; my beloved,
in whom my soul is well pleased: I will put my spirit
upon him, and he shall shew judgment to the Gentiles.
                            Matthew 12:18

If we have a spirit, then He has a Spirit. Most Christians assume that the spirit that is within us is God's Spirit. But the Spirit of God bears witness with our spirit. So, the spirit within you is *your* spirit. My soul within me is *my* soul, and my body is *my* body.

It is our desire to be like Jesus, but we fall short more often than we care to admit. I never realized this until God revealed it to me. I thought that when I gave my life to God, His Spirit came into me. Well, it did, but only in the places where I allowed it to reign. The places where I denied Him still had to be dealt with. The holes in your soul are the places where we have rejected God's presence (the dry places). I have scripture to back up this revelation. David told God:

Create in me a clean heart, O God; and renew a right
spirit within me. Cast me not away from thy presence;
and take not thy holy spirit from me. Restore unto me
the joy of thy salvation; and uphold me with thy free
spirit.   Psalm 51:10-12

31

In other words, David's spirit was wrong and needed to be healed. Even David had soul holes. Psalm 51:10 is probably one of the most powerful prayers a person can pray, *"Lord, create in me a clean heart and renew a right spirit in me."* If your heart is unclean, then your spirit will be wrong.

Have you ever seen a Christian "show their butt"? In South Georgia, when we say "show your butt," we don't mean it literally. It is slang for "pitch a fit" or "make a tail out of yourself" (for lack of better words). This place of fit pitching is a hole in your soul that hasn't allowed your spirit to line up with the Spirit of God. Therefore, wherever the soul hole presides, the presence of God cannot reside. God is gentle and will not go where He is not fully accepted. The only way we can truly have the Spirit of God within us is when we come into agreement with His precious Holy Spirit. When God's glory fills our soul hole, it becomes whole. Instead of your soul hole being an indention, it can be filled by God with an intention.

Have you ever considered how a sponge works? Loose fibers in the sponge create empty spaces. The holes between the fibers soak up water and swell. This prevents the water from sloshing back out of the sponge. Instead, the water is trapped inside until the sponge is squeezed.

Another interesting point is that the fuller the sponge becomes the heavier it gets. Imagine your soul full of holes as a result of past pains. Through soul searching and repenting, God fills your soul holes. The empty space that pain once occupied is now a hole for God to reside in. Once saturated in His presence, you begin to swell with His goodness and become subdued by His *kavod* presence. *Kavod* is the Hebrew word for *glory:*

If God gave us a body, then He has a body:

> *And the Word was made flesh, and dwelt among us,*
> *(and we beheld his glory, the glory as of the only begot-*
> *ten of the Father,) full of grace and truth.*   John 1:14

God has given us the ability to receive all that He is, with the exception of the deception that came through the conception of humanistic fallibility. In other words, we can be like our Heavenly Father, but we still have to deal with our fallible ways. We were conceived in sin in our mother's womb:

> *Behold, I was shapen in iniquity; and in sin did my*
> *mother conceive me.*   Psalm 51:5

This information comes to us just a few scriptures before David speaks about having an unclean heart and stating that he needed a right spirit. If it were not enough that we shared the womb with sin, we also came from our father's loins, thus inheriting generational curses:

> *Keeping mercy for thousands, forgiving iniquity and*
> *transgression and sin, and that will by no means clear*
> *the guilty; visiting the iniquity of the fathers upon the*
> *children, and upon the children's children, unto the third*
> *and to the fourth generation.*   Exodus 34:7

In our mother's womb, we shared our space with sin that came in from the loins of our father through the iniquities of our forefathers. No wonder we have soul holes! These indentions (soul holes) may be because of our ancestors and the traditions and teachings of their dysfunctions.

Because of the Fall of man, God sent His seed through the womb of a virgin, who had never been contaminated by man's seed. In other words, God bypassed man to bring forth His sinless Son. God sent Truth to the earth to be planted in the soil (womb) of a virgin, and He did it to give life to all men. God sent His only begotten Son to the earth to be crucified for our sins. The Truth Seed that God sowed had to die in order for Truth to be planted in the soil (womb) of the earth. A seed must die to bring forth life:

> *Verily, verily, I say unto you, Except a corn of wheat fall into the ground and die, it abideth alone: but if it die, it bringeth forth much fruit.* John 12:24

The flawless Seed of God entered into an untouched woman, to be buried in a borrowed tomb in the earth's soil. Notice the similarities of the words *womb* and *tomb*.

After the resurrection, Jesus left the earth realm, so that the Holy Spirit could come as a Comforter to us, as we walk out our own salvation. He said that He would not leave us comfortless:

> *I will not leave you comfortless: I will come to you.* John 14:18

> *Nevertheless I tell you the truth; It is expedient for you that I go away: for if I go not away, the Comforter will*

not come unto you; but if I depart, I will send him unto
you. John 16:7

The only way back to the father is through Jesus Christ, the Son, because He offers the only sinless route back to the Father:

Jesus saith unto him, I am the way, the truth, and
the life: no man cometh unto the Father, but by me.
John 14:6

Through Jesus, we too have the triunity of eternity operating in our DNA.

I would like to share an illustration that represents the totality of eternity. If the trinity is three-in-one, then when divided into thirds, we see an equality of the trinity demonstrated. Thirty-three point three percent represents the Father, thirty-three point three percent represents the Son, and thirty-three point three percent represents the Holy Spirit. When added up, the total comes to ninety-nine point nine, which is point one percent away from one hundred percent or wholeness. The point one percent that is missing from the equation is *you:*

How think ye? if a man have an hundred sheep, and
one of them be gone astray, doth he not leave the
ninety and nine, and goeth into the mountains, and
seeketh that which is gone astray? And if so be that
he find it, verily I say unto you, he rejoiceth more of
that sheep, than of the ninety and nine which went

not astray. Even so it is not the will of your Father which is in heaven, that one of these little ones should perish. Matthew 18:12-14

God is infinite; therefore, Jesus and the Holy Spirit are infinite as well. When infinite is divided by 3, it remains infinite. God, Jesus, and the Holy Spirit are 3 in 1. When divided equally, it calculates to 33.3 per entity. The remaining factor is .1 percent to make a 100% wholeness. The .1 is you; therefore, you become infinite.

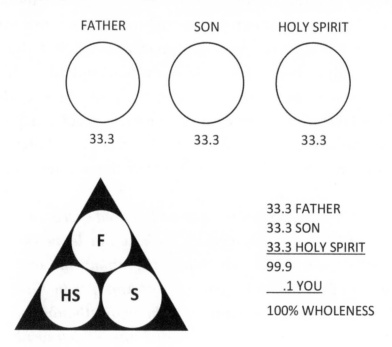

33.3 FATHER
33.3 SON
<u>33.3 HOLY SPIRIT</u>
99.9
<u>   .1 YOU</u>
100% WHOLENESS

I think it is very interesting that Jesus was thirty-three years old when He was crucified.

We must be able to discern the difference in all three aspects. Each aspect of our individuality should be equally analyzed. When soul holes are present, they dominate and dictate the other two aspects of humanity. The *soul* is the one aspect that is in the balance, because the spirit goes back from whence it came, and the body goes back to the dust:

> *Then shall the dust return to the earth as it was:*
> *and the spirit shall return unto God who gave it.*
> Ecclesiastes 12:7

The spirit, body, and soul all operate in unison, but we need to be able to separate their functions to be able to understand and identify each aspect. We need, not only to understand their functions, but also their dysfunctions. It is difficult to separate the body, soul, and spirit, because they were intended to operate corporately, as a whole. The truth is that if the soul has holes, it cannot function as a whole. Wholeness comes as a result of getting our soul holes filled. When we have a lack of knowledge concerning soul holes, we fall prey to the holes in our souls. If we don't understand the holes in our souls, then eventually holes will start to show up in our bodies.

According to the word of God in Hebrews 4:12, we can separate the spirit, soul, and body:

> *For the word of God is quick, and powerful, and*
> *sharper than any twoedged sword, piercing even*

to the dividing asunder of soul and spirit, and of the joints and marrow, and is a discerner of the thoughts and intents of the heart.

Many Christians are fearful when I teach them to consider identifying the spirit, body, and soul individually. Relax! It is fear that keeps you in bondage to your brokenness, which is better known as your fear soul holes. This fear comes because New Age religion has done this very thing, without giving Jesus Christ the glory. If it has worked for them, then how much better will it work for us when we apply the Holy Scriptures and walk in truth.

I have friends who practice New Age, and they have much more peace, joy, and prosperity than most Christians I know. The missing piece of the puzzle is Jesus Christ. If you are a Christian, you have Jesus, and you can boldly analyze all three aspects of our humanistic makeup. You can get healed, and then give God more glory and praise than ever before. You cannot truly give God all the glory until you are free.

Remember, it is the truth that can set you free. Fear is an excuse that keeps you in ignorance and bondage. There is a prayer I pray when God tries to show me something new that I have never seen before:

I RECEIVE ALL GOOD AND REJECT ALL EVIL!

There are no new things under the sun. It is not new to God; it is just new to me! I don't fear things that I do not know; I fear not knowing the things that God desires to show me. Take a leap of faith and open yourself to see the unknown ways of God. The reason they are unknown is because Christians fear the unknown. Why do we automatically reject the things we don't know? It is the hidden mysteries of God's glory that He desires to reveal:

> *Even the mystery which hath been hid from ages and from generations, but now is made manifest to his saints.* Colossians 1:26

We must stop denying the truth of God, whether we are aware of it or not, and be open to seeking and finding the hidden mysteries of eternity, while we are here on earth. He has said:

> *My people are destroyed for lack of knowledge: because thou hast rejected knowledge, I will also reject thee, that thou shalt be no priest to me: seeing thou hast forgotten the law of thy God, I will also forget thy children.* Hosea 4:6

In this case, fear would be not knowing how to get our soul holes healed. We can be set free only when we come into this soul-hole knowledge. Knowledge is power. Many people desire God's power without having to learn His knowledge. But learning the knowledge of God comes with experiencing God's presence.

Many people in church today know the Word of God without knowing the presence of God. This can be dangerous, and I see many leaders causing more damage than good. Leaders can have soul holes too. If soul holes are not healed, we teach our children (congregation) out of our brokenness.

It is easy to ignore your soul holes because it takes effort to get set free. Sometimes it is just easier to act like you are all right, when you are really dying on the inside because of your soul holes. I have seen many people succumb to a premature death because their soul holes became deeper and wider with age, without them understanding the indenting interruptions in their soul. It seemed easier to die than to change.

Here's a good analogy: when your body becomes broken, you take it to the doctor to get it fixed. This is easy because you are expecting someone else to fix it. We expect the doctor to work miracles, yet we are not willing to work miracles ourselves by taking accountability for our brokenness. When we understand soul holes, it will be easier for us to find our healing.

The spirit and soul make up the inner man, so issues in this area are easier to hide than physical issues in the body. The symptoms show up in the body because the soul has holes, which are often ignored. Tuning up our spirits and souls is a little more complex than putting a cast on a broken arm. The goal is to get anything that is broken made whole.

It would be simple if we could take our broken souls into a garage to get a tune-up every three thousand miles like we do our cars. By the way, the people who were afraid that this was a form of New Age have been the most impacted by this concept. Here is a statement that has helped me to stop being so "stiff-necked" about this whole matter:

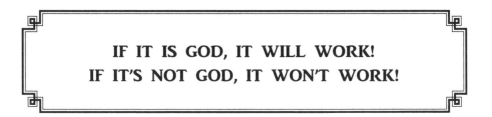

IF IT IS GOD, IT WILL WORK!
IF IT'S NOT GOD, IT WON'T WORK!

But if it be of God, ye cannot overthrow it; lest haply ye be found even to fight against God.

Acts 5:39

Don't sweat the small stuff. Believe and trust God to work out all of the details. I can see a clear insight into afflictions when soul holes are identified. We have many unidentified fear soul holes, as we fear getting involved in things that are not of the Lord. If that be the case, then why don't we do something with our bad habits and attitudes? We should not let the lack of exponential knowledge rob us from being made whole. God wants to do a new thing within us that will consist of our doing a new thing! If you want different you must do different:

Behold, I will do a new thing; now it shall spring forth; shall ye not know it? I will even make a way in the wilderness, and rivers in the desert.

Isaiah 43:19

41

Preparation for a New Thing

We know that the Bible says that there is no new thing under the sun. Therefore, what we desire to see come to pass is ancient:

> *The thing that hath been, it is that which shall be;*
> *and that which is done is that which shall be done:*
> *and there is no new thing under the sun.*
>
> Ecclesiastes 1:9

If there is no new thing under the sun that hath been done, that means we must do a new thing. We must abandon our old ways, change, and be available to do new things.

We desire a new way because we desire demonstrations. As the remnant, we must prepare ourselves to become holy through the glory of God, so that we can experience this fulfillment of the last-day dispensation:

> *In that day shall the Lord of hosts be for a crown of*
> *glory, and for a diadem of beauty, unto the residue*
> *of his people.*
>
> Isaiah 28:5

Are you interested in becoming a part of a people (remnant) whom God desires to use to bring forth the REST of HIS GLORY, on Earth as it is in Heaven? Rest, in itself, would be a demonstrated miracle for many Christians. Rest is the evidence of depth. We must rest in order to see the rest of God. There awaits a remnant of people who shall rest in God's glory and not have to taste death. They will be an

Elijah Generation that will go up in a blaze of God's glory and supersede death:

> *And it came to pass, as they still went on, and talked, that, behold, there appeared a chariot of fire, and horses of fire, and parted them both asunder; and Elijah went up by a whirlwind into heaven.*
>
> 2 Kings 2:11

This is a remnant that will possess the rest of Hebrews 4. The whole fourth chapter of Hebrews talks about this remnant. If you are interested in being the remnant, you might want to read it. Rest may be the new thing that God is desiring to spring up in you in this hour. "Drivenness," which is performance, is the indented evidence of soul holes. We will be discussing drivenness later in the book.

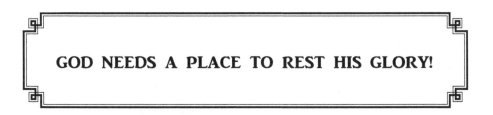

GOD NEEDS A PLACE TO REST HIS GLORY!

> *For the word of God is quick, and powerful, and sharper than any twoedged sword, piercing even to the dividing asunder of soul and spirit, and of the joints and marrow, and is a discerner of the thoughts and intents of the heart.* Hebrews 4:12

This passage of scripture is the only one that I can find concerning the dividing of the soul, the spirit, and the body. As a matter of fact, the body is recognized here only by way of inner joints and marrow. The joints are another deeper level than the outward appearance. This is an analogy of going deeper into the body.

The marrow is an even deeper dimension of the inner man. The marrow holds the life of the bones. The Body of Christ must go deeper to experience this place of wholeness.

This scripture goes beyond the outward appearance of the body into the deeper places, the joints and marrow. It illustrates to us that there is always a deeper resting place that God is calling His sons and daughters to come into. Jesus introduced us to this place in Matthew 16:28:

> *Verily I say unto you, There are some standing here, which shall not taste of death, till they see the Son of man coming in his kingdom.*

The depth of rest that God is ushering His remnant into is a rest without death. We must be able to go to the depths of our spirit, soul, and body and walk in authority, if we are to see the Kingdom of God come to pass. (I explain more about this in a pamphlet called "Oh Death, Where Is Thy Sting"?).

When we consider the body, we usually only consider the outer portion, the shell. This is true when it comes to our issues. If we can make everything look good on the outside, we will not have to deal with what is on the inside. Jesus dealt with people that had this mentality. Unfortunately, it was the religious sects:

> *Woe unto you, scribes and Pharisees, hypocrites!*
> *for ye make clean the outside of the cup and of the*
> *platter, but within they are full of extortion and*
> *excess.*   Matthew 23:25

Be careful not to be religious and stay on the outer surface only. We must go in deep, in order to get to the root, so that the truth can set us free. We want to go through the fruit, back down to the branch, to the trunk, and right down to the root, to get to the truth, so that we can become the seed that God intended us to be. I have *seed* the glory of the coming of the Lord. Lighten up a little bit. We have a whole book to get through together.

The body is made up of dust. Therefore, we experience dry places in our lives (see Genesis 2:7). Have you ever experienced a spiritual, mental, emotional, physical, relational, or financial dry place? God did not create us to be dry. We became dry when, in disobedience, our ancestors walked away from the center of the garden. In the midst of God's mist, everyone and everything was saturated with God's presence:

> *But there went up a mist from the earth, and wa-*
> *tered the whole face of the ground.*   Genesis 2:6

Do you want to be the whole face of the ground or do you just want to be a piece of dirt? There was no need for rain in the garden because God reigned. God communed with Adam and Eve in the cool of the day. Why was it in the cool of the day? God loves us so much that He wants us to be cool! I am presently sitting outside in the sun, and suddenly, a cloud and a breeze have come over me. God is so good to me.

God came up as a mist, in the midst of the garden, to be with Adam and Eve. After the fall, God created us to be vessels so that we could become full of His presence:

> *He that believeth on me, as the scripture hath said, out of his belly shall flow rivers of living water.*
>
> John 7:38

I see a clear parallel in the Word of God between the Spirit and water. Remember, our spirit was with God before the foundation of the world. I would like to share with you a few more scriptures that confirm that water represents God's spirit:

> *But whosoever drinketh of the water that I shall give him shall never thirst; but the water that I shall give him shall be in him a well of water springing up into everlasting life.*
>
> John 4:14

> *The glory of this latter house shall be greater than of the former, saith the LORD of hosts: and in this place will I give peace, saith the LORD of hosts.*
>
> Haggai 2:9

For the earth shall be filled with the knowledge of the glory of the LORD as the waters cover the sea.

Habakkuk 2:14

Therefore with joy shall ye draw water out of the wells of salvation.

Isaiah 12:3

And the earth was without form, and void; and darkness was upon the face of the deep. And the Spirit of God moved upon the face of the waters.

Genesis 1:2

In order to understand the comparison between water and God's Spirit, we must learn that we are the earth in need of God's saturation. Seventy percent of the earth is covered in water. Land makes up the other thirty percent. We call the water *"a body of water."* Land surrounded by a body of water is an island. We is the land (IS LAND)! The promise is real, is you real (Is-real)? God is still looking for His true sons and daughters to be real.

Seventy percent represents our spiritual, and the thirty percent represents our natural land man (soul and body). When all three aspects are considered, 70% represents the spirit, 15% represents the body, and 15% represents the soul. It is our land man that becomes dry, not our spirit man. The earth/land ratio is confirmation that the land (natural) is the only part of a man that can be dry.

70% SPIRIT (SPIRIT MAN)
15 % BODY (LAND MAN)
15% SOUL (LAND MAN)

Paul calls us an earthen vessel with treasures:

But we have this treasure in earthen vessels, that the excellency of the power may be of God, and not of us.   2 Corinthians 4:7

If we are the earthen vessel that has treasures, then we must open our chest (soul) and get healed from all the soul holes that try to keep us closed. If we have holes in our souls and have not become whole, then when God pours Himself into us, the glory will leak out of us. When we have holes, we close. If we close, we will not allow anyone to get close. God desires to bless us abundantly, but we cannot receive His blessings if our souls cannot contain the blessings because of the holes.

We also see a parallel in 2 Chronicles 7:14 to the earth (land) that needs to be healed:

If my people, which are called by my name, shall humble themselves, and pray, and seek my face, and turn from their wicked ways; then will I hear from heaven, and will forgive their sin, and will heal their land.   2 Chronicles 7:14

This is evidence that my land man (soul and body) needs to be healed. The land man is the only part of you that can be dry. The spirit is represented as water, and water can never be dry.

Another parallel is found in the beginning when the earth was void and without form:

> *In the beginning God created the heaven and the earth. And the earth was without form, and void; and darkness was upon the face of the deep. And the Spirit of God moved upon the face of the waters.*
>
> Genesis 1:1-2

Our souls are void and without form as long as they have soul holes. We are the earth that is in need of healing, and as soon as we realize this, then (and only then) will our soul holes be able to be filled, so that the glory of God can make us whole.

We are the earth that was without form and void. Therefore, God will fill up our emptiness as the waters cover the sea. When He fills us up as the waters cover the sea, then we will be able to see wholly.

I once saw an upside-down rainbow, and I courageously asked God, "What is this?"

He said, "It's a rainbow."

I said, "I know it's a rainbow, but why is it upside down?"

He said, "It's not upside down from where I sit. Did you not ask Me to allow you to see like I see? From where I sit, it's a smile."

Wow! Never in my life had I imagined seeing an upside-down rainbow. When we make ourselves available to hear and see from God, He will show us and tell us things that we have never imagined.

Several weeks later, I said to God, "Is there anything more beautiful than an upside-down rainbow?"

He said, "Oh, Yeah!" When I looked up into the sky, there was a double upside-down rainbow. To God be all the glory! There is always more, and it is up to us how much we seek the "more."

If you want to see a little, seek a little. If you want to see a lot, seek a lot. If you want to see the King, keep see-king.

We also see a parallel in being the land and God's glory filling us and fulfilling His Word:

> *Every valley shall be exalted, and every mountain and hill shall be made low: and the crooked shall be made straight, and the rough places plain.* Isaiah 40:4

We are the land that God desires to fill, and He can only fill those who allow His glory to arise in this hour as the waters cover the sea. This is why it is so important to have the knowledge of the glory. If the glory is what is going to fill us as the waters cover the sea, then in order to be filled, we must know what the glory of God is. When we get filled, we get healed.

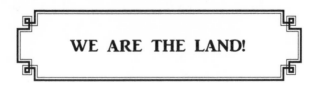

WE ARE THE LAND!

When the land becomes dry, it is because of a lack of rain. When a church becomes dry, it is because of the lack of God's presence (reign). Do you see the parallel? Water is an element that mankind cannot live without. I once read a book entitled, *You're Not Sick, You're Thirsty*.[2] There is healing in the water. God once told me that water was His liquid love.

Water is tasteless. In other words, it is less desirable than other drinks, which contain sweet additives, but it is the only substance that can truly quench your thirst. Drinks that have additives just make you thirstier.

Water is pure, and it flows freely from the earth's core. Water is the only substance that will penetrate the earth with provision in order to turn its ashes into beauty. Water has the potential to sustain life both in the earth and in the body. Water is one of the last desired substances on earth before one tastes death. Water and blood are also the two elements that we were formed in while we were still in our mother's womb:

> *For thou hast possessed my reins: thou hast covered me in my mother's womb.*   Psalm 139:13

Notice the word *rein*! The dictionary defines *rein* as a "restraining influence." The Fall of man restrained our reign. Therefore, God had to let it rain to restore His reign, on Earth as it is in Heaven. The latter rain will be even greater than the former rain.

---

2. Batmangheldj, F., MD, New York, NY, Warner Books:2003

Break down the word restrain and you have REST and RAIN. When we rest in God, His reign can come and saturate us with His presence.

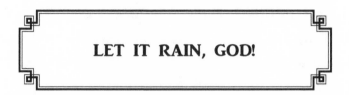

LET IT RAIN, GOD!

Water seeks its own level and floods first to the deepest, emptiest places. That sounds like God's Spirit, doesn't it? His Spirit fills the deepest, emptiest soul holes of His sons and daughters.

Soul holes are the voids, without form, the empty places mentioned in Genesis 1.

Water is a universal solvent. Think about what would happen if you placed a steel beam into the sea for one year. The salt water would dissolve the beam. God desires to dissolve the things in your soul that are eating you alive and stealing your joy.

If water represents God's Spirit and our soul has holes, then how will this affect our Christian lives? Have you ever been to a great service and been filled with the presence of God, only to find yourself empty again the next day? This is where the knowledge of soul holes can set you free. God filled you, but your soul holes allowed the presence of God to seep out of you like a bag with holes in it. You were hoping that you would be different, but as reality hit you, you realized that you were as empty as you had been before you were filled. Holes in your soul will not allow your soul to contain the presence of God that you desire. When you get your soul holes filled, then you will awaken to the reality of your wholeness.

When you become whole, then you become holy. This is when you will be able to go to work and minister to your co-workers out of your abundance and not your emptiness. We are supposed to pour ourselves out to others so they can partake of the living water that is within us. Paul said it best:

> *But even if I am being poured out as a drink offering on the sacrifice and service of your faith [for preaching the message of salvation], still I rejoice and share my joy with you all.* Philippians 2:17, AMP

When your soul holes are filled, you live out of your wholeness. God is so cool. He created our bodies with pores because He called us to pour ourselves out to others in love. If you have helped many people in your brokenness, how many more people can you impact in your wholeness? We cannot be poured out if we are empty.

Dear Heavenly Father,

Thank You for sharing this insight and revelation about soul holes. I ask that You continue to give me understanding about what lies inside of my soul. I desire to be set free and made whole. Teach me how to come out of agreement with the dry places and saturate my soul with

Your presence. Unveil me from the lies that try to hide in my soul. Holy Spirit, speak Your words of truth and bring forth understanding for my unveiling.

In Jesus' name!

CHAPTER 2

BE YE HOLY, NOT HOLEY

Because it is written: Be ye holy, for I am holy.

1 Peter 1:16

Make no qualms about it, God is calling us to be the temple of His Spirit:

> *Know ye not that ye are the temple of God, and that the Spirit of God dwelleth in you?*
>
> 1 Corinthians 3:16

For those of us who are interested in becoming the temple, God is preparing us, as we get our soul holes filled. God did not say, "Be ye holey." He said "Be ye HOLY." In order to be the temple, we must first get our soul holes healed, for the temple is holy. The goal is to be holy, not holey!

The counterfeit to being holy is being full of holes. The difference between being the Church and being the Temple is simple: The church is only filled with people once or twice a week, whereas the Temple is filled twenty-four seven with God's glory. This is why, in order to be filled, it is important to know the glory. You can't be filled with something that you have no knowledge of. The truth is that the glory of God is already in you. You just have to let it arise.

Jesus bore holes in His hands and feet for our holes in our souls to be filled with His glory. It is the glory of God that fills your soul holes. In other words, you must be filled (flooded) with God's glory, so that it goes over the walls of self-protection which you have erected around your soul:

> *So shall they fear the name of the LORD from the west, and his glory from the rising of the sun. When the enemy shall come in like a flood, the Spirit of the LORD shall lift up a standard against him.*
>
> Isaiah 59:19

We automatically assume that the enemy is the devil. The truth is that the evil (d-evil) is in me, (enemy, IN-A-ME). Point to your heart and say, "In-a-me." As the glory arises within you, it spills over the walls of self-protection which are around your soul and goes first straight to your deepest, emptiest soul holes. Everything that you have need of is already in you because God made you. These emptiest places are usually identified as fear, rejection, and abandonment. We are the "earth" that is to be filled with God's glory.

THE DIFFERENCE BETWEEN BEING THE CHURCH AND BEING THE TEMPLE IS SIMPLE!

Many churches do not know about the glory of God. Some do not desire to know the glory because the glory is what changes a person. If the glory of God is present, then mankind has no itinerary. Most people do not want to change. Some leaders do not want their people to change because change brings change. It is sad to say that some leaders do not want their flock to get healed because they would no longer have slaves. People have become settlers in their serious situations and have gotten stuck in the mundane madness of their own imaginations. The church is made up of settlers, but the temple is made up of pioneers that explore the hidden mysteries of God's will.

Don't settle with your soul holes. With God's glory, explore the different avenues of adventure and be made whole. Settlers find a place and grow roots. Explorers possess greater possibilities and seek roots in the Truth, thus having their holes filled. This consists of pulling up any roots of untruths.

Churches sing about the glory, but they do not have the knowledge of the glory. I believe that one of the reasons our country is so blessed is because our national flag is called "Old Glory." The red stripes on Old Glory represent the stripes Jesus bore for us to make us free. The white stripes represent the healing of the nations that will come forth out of America's obedience to God. The blue represents the Spirit of God, and the stars represents the descendants of Abraham.

Abraham went out, not knowing where he was going. I believe that Abraham's offspring (that will be as great as the stars in the sky) discovered America:

> *And I will make thy seed to multiply as the stars of heaven, and will give unto thy seed all these countries; and in thy seed shall all the nations of the earth be blessed.*   Genesis 26:4

Do we really understand why our country is so blessed? We are a little Israel. Israel does not need America; America needs Israel. I cannot go into this much because it is a book within itself, but America is blessed because America is playing a vital role in the fulfillment of prophecy. America will be the catalyst that ushers in the glory, as our nation experiences the glory arising from sea to shining sea.

Take a fresh look at the words of our anthem. These words have been declared over America since 1814. The first words are, "*O say can you see?*" Say, can *you* see what God is saying?

> *"O say can you see, by the dawn's early light,*
> *What so proudly we hail'd at the twilight's last gleaming,*
> *Whose broad stripes and bright stars through the perilous fight*
> *O'er the ramparts we watch'd were so gallantly streaming?*

58

And the rocket's red glare, the bombs bursting in
air,
Gave proof through the night that our flag was
still there,
O say does that star-spangled banner yet wave
O'er the land of the free and the home of the brave?

On the shore dimly seen through the mists of the
deep
Where the foe's haughty host in dread silence re-
poses,
What is that which the breeze, o'er the towering
steep,
As it fitfully blows, half conceals, half discloses?
Now it catches the gleam of the morning's first
beam,
In full glory reflected now shines in the stream,
'Tis the star-spangled banner - O long may it wave
O'er the land of the free and the home of the brave!

And where is that band who so vauntingly swore,
That the havoc of war and the battle's confusion
A home and a Country should leave us no more?
Their blood has wash'd out their foul footstep's
pollution.
No refuge could save the hireling and slave
From the terror of flight or the gloom of the grave,
And the star-spangled banner in triumph doth wave
O'er the land of the free and the home of the brave.

O thus be it ever when freemen shall stand
Between their lov'd home and the war's desolation!
Blest with vict'ry and peace may the heav'n rescued
land
Praise the power that hath made and preserv'd us
a nation!
Then conquer we must, when our cause it is just,
And this be our motto - "In God is our trust,"
And the star-spangled banner in triumph shall
wave.
O'er the land of the free and the home of the brave."[3]

The Land of the Free sounds like an eternal declaration made over a land that would see to it that God receives all the glory. The glory of God has been declared over America since her inception. Unfortunately, the majority of Americans have no knowledge of the last three verses of this amazing declaration. This is a great example of knowing only a quarter of the truth and not allowing all of it to set you free. Is your land free?

We are the land, but are we free? Do you know the whole truth, or have you only known a quarter of the truth? We must know the whole truth in order to be set free. We must have the knowledge of the glory of God before our land can be set free. I can confess that my land is not free, but I desire to be free.

First, I have to admit that I am not free before I start my process of being set free. God desires a remnant of people to know His glory so that He can bring forth the rest of His story (HISTORY).

---

3. Francis Scott Key

The glory brings the whole truth. The knowledge of the glory has to cover the earth as the waters cover the sea, but it has to start with you and me. You have to pay the price to be free. Jesus paid the price for us, but we must make ourselves available by sacrificing our selfishness, so that we can receive what Jesus did for us on the cross.

When I talk about generational curses, legalistic people say, "Well, Jesus paid it all on the cross that day." He did pay it all, and if he hadn't, none of us would be here today. But this is not an excuse to remain in bondage.

If Jesus paid it all, then why do we have mortgage payments? You see, we really don't believe that Jesus paid it all, or we all would be debt free (even as a nation). God is teaching us through His truth: there is a place where we can be free—mentally, spiritually, physically, and financially debt free. It must start with US. You are the land, and God wants US (United States) to be totally free.

In other words, a veteran who has paid the price of war will know more about the anthem than a millennial. Maybe we are not as free as we could be because we haven't paid the price yet. I want to pay the price and get it right, so I can walk in the land of the free.

I am thankful that God chose me to live in the USA and that I have the privilege of living under Old Glory, which represents my nation.

I pledge allegiance to the flag of the United States of America and to the Republic for which it stands,

one nation under God, indivisible, with liberty and justice for all.

GLORY TO GOD, AMERICA IS A LITTLE ISRAEL!

The "new glory" could be what God desires to do in us. We must release the old glory to see the new come forth on our land. Could it be that God has to do it in us before He can do it in the US? Religious and political traditions have tried to pervert the truth of God, but the gates of Hell will not prevail:

> *And I say also unto thee, That thou art Peter, and upon this rock I will build my church; and the gates of hell shall not prevail against it.* Matthew 16:18

It is not a red or blue matter; it's a TRUTH matter. You (U) are the center of TRUTH. The truth must be the center of you in order for you to be free. The glory is filling this earth so that mankind can come into the holiness of God. The USA plays a vital role in the glory of the Lord filling the earth as the waters cover the sea. The letters USA can be found in the center of the name *JERUSALEM*. The United States of America is abbreviated as U.S. This is a clear sign that it is US. We are the ones who can be filled with the knowledge of the glory of the Lord in the land of the free. And those who are free will be the ones who carry the glory of God. They are a people filled with His glory. They are the temple of the Holy Spirit.[4]

The glory has an assignment of its own, and that is to allow God to have His way. As the glory fills the earth, then it will make us whole, instead of void and without form. When you call forth the glory of God, chances are you are not going to have a traditional service or a traditional life. You will not be interested in following the crowd; you will be focused on following the cloud of God's presence.

People like to be in control. Therefore, the glory of God cramps their style. If you want to do life your way, chances are you will not carry much of the glory of God. It is either your way or Yahweh. Signs, wonders, and miracles come forth in the glory, which is what we need to be healed. This is why we are not seeing many miracles in churches these days. In order to see the miraculous, we must carry the holiness of God (Yahweh). If we want more of God, then we have to make room in our souls, by getting our soul holes made whole. God needs us to be His temple, so He can fill us with His glory.

I love to sit and talk to the old-timers about the tabernacle days. Tabernacles were the places where sawdust covered the ground under a rusted tin roof, and wood stoves warmed the bodies of those seeking the fire of God. After hours of worship (without sound boards, lighting, or acoustics), the glory cloud would come into the tabernacle. As a result of the glory cloud,

---

4. I have written more about the temple in my upcoming book, **Dispensations of God's Glory.**

salvations, healings, and deliverances would saturate the God seekers. As of old, the glory of God is what filled the temple:

> *It came even to pass, as the trumpeters and singers were as one, to make one sound to be heard in praising and thanking the Lord; and when they lifted up their voice with the trumpets and cymbals and instruments of musick, and praised the Lord, saying, For he is good; for his mercy endureth for ever: that then the house was filled with a cloud, even the house of the Lord; so that the priests could not stand to minister by reason of the cloud: for the glory of the Lord had filled the house of God.*
>
> 2 Chronicles 5:13-14

The main reason people do not understand the glory of God is that they are consumed with walking in their own glory. You cannot carry God's glory while walking in your own glory:

> *I am the Lord: that is my name: and my glory will I not give to another, neither my praise to graven images.*   Isaiah 42:8

God makes it very clear in this passage that He will not give His glory to another. The evidence of vainglory is still expecting God to bless us when we choose to walk in our own ways instead of His. *Vainglory* is "excessive vanity or inordinate pride in oneself or one's achievements." Vainglory is the translation of *kendoxia,* which is empty glory or pride. Pulpits today are full of sermons taught as the evidence of an individual's intellect instead of demonstrations of eternity. If your life is empty, vainglory can be the soul hole that makes you miserable and bitter. In other words, God will let you do things your way as long as you want to.

Here are a few scriptures that describe vainglory:

> *Let nothing be done through strife or vainglory; but in lowliness of mind let each esteem other better than themselves.* Philippians 2:3

> *Let us not be desirous of vain glory, provoking one another, envying one another.* Galatians 5:26

> *For all that is in the world, the lust of the flesh, and the lust of the eyes, and the pride of life, is not of the Father, but is of the world.* 1 John 2:16

Pride usually accompanies vainglory, while humility accompanies God's glory. God's glory brings an ease to life and expedites eternity on earth. You will never be the same after you begin to learn of God's glory, but one must trade in the vanities of humanity to make himself available for that glory.

The glory of God is mentioned three hundred and ninety-seven times in the Word of God. The glory is the unexplained, convincing, manifested presence of God. It is the cloud by day and the fire by night:

And the LORD went before them by day in a pillar of a cloud, to lead them the way; and by night in a pillar of fire, to give them light; to go by day and night.   Exodus 13:21

In order to get your soul holes filled, you must have the knowledge of the glory of God. It is the knowledge of the glory of the Lord that fills the earth (you and me) as the waters cover the sea. We must have knowledge of the glory in order to be filled.

Dear Father God,

I purpose and choose with my free will to repent for any ways that I haven't acknowledged Your glory. According to Your Word, the whole earth is filled with Your glory. Forgive me for the ways that I have not given You the glory for the many blessings in my life. I am beginning to understand that I was made with Your glory, by Your glory, and for Your glory. Thank You for teaching me about Your glory and filling my soul holes with Your glory. God, show me Your glory!

Amen!

SHOW ME YOUR GLORY

We must have the glory of God in order to be the temple of the Lord. Moses saw the glory in the burning bush on the "backside of nowhere":

Now Moses kept the flock of Jethro his father in law, the priest of Midian: and he led the flock to the backside of the desert, and came to the mountain of God, even to Horeb. And the angel of the Lord appeared unto him in a flame of fire out of the midst of a bush: and he looked, and, behold, the bush burned with fire, and the bush was not consumed. Exodus 3:1-2

I wonder how Moses felt on the "backside of nowhere," while tending to someone else's business. (This sounds like the lives of most of the church).

Mount Horeb means *desolation*, so this tells us that he was in a desolate place. In order to see and hear God's glory, you must be desperate. Moses was about eighty years old, so surely he thought his season was over. Suddenly, the glory appeared, and he turned to see why the bush was not consumed. Moses could have said, "Oh, well, it's just a burning bush," but he turned and examined the bush carefully. In other words, the glory got Moses' attention. He said:

And Moses said, I will now turn aside, and see this great sight, why the bush is not burnt. And when the LORD saw that he turned aside to see, God called unto him out of the midst of the bush, and said, Moses, Moses. And he said, Here am I. Exodus 3:3-4

The reason God used Moses mightily was because he turned, and he changed. Moses was desperate to see God's glory. He was sick and tired of being sick and tired:

And he said, I beseech thee, shew me thy glory.
Exodus 33:18

Turning from our ways is what is needed in our individual lives and in America as a whole. If you desire a paradigm shift, start praying this prayer:

God, show me Your glory!

Dear Father God,

Please forgive me for all of the ways I have operated in vainglory, for it has kept me from walking in Your glory. I forgive myself, and I ask You to forgive me for allowing my selfish ways to overtake Your way of truth. Lord, I have spent much of my life walking in my own desolate vainglorious ways and have procrastinated about following Your way for my life. I have been foolish when it comes to vanity, and for this I ask for Your grace and mercy to cover me. I forgive all others for teaching me their vainglory and expecting me to walk in their ways. Lord, show me Your glory so that my soul holes will be filled, and I will be able to complete every assignment You have created me for in this earth realm.

In Jesus' name,
Amen!

God's glory desires to show us things that we have longed to experience our whole lives. Soul holes have kept us from experiencing the true intimacy of God's glory. When we get our soul holes filled, we can come out of agreement with a desolate destiny and be able to fulfill our earthly assignment.

It is never too late to see our heart's desires come to pass, on Earth as it is in Heaven. We just need to become holy, to turn from our holes, and to get filled with God's glory. No matter what season of time we are in, we must turn from the ways that our soul holes have lied to us, and we must make ourselves available to be set free.

Moses' soul holes had to be filled before he could be used to set the Israelites free from their bondage. Only the free can set other captives free. In other words, Moses had to deal with his fear, rejection, and abandonment issues before God could use him to fulfill his destiny. His destiny consisted of setting an entire nation free.

Just as Moses had no idea how greatly God desired to use him, you have no idea how greatly God desires to use you. Stop procrastinating about your destiny and fulfill it by dealing with your soul holes. Who knows? God may use you to set a nation free. This is why the Bible says we have to come as children:

> *And said, Verily I say unto you, Except ye be converted, and become as little children, ye shall not enter into the kingdom of heaven.*   Matthew 18:3

As a child, your soul was not yet full of holes. It was still holy from being with the Father. As we get older, negative emotions and traumas set in, and our souls fall prey to our being set in our ways, which causes pain. As pain sets in, a pathway is created within us that places us in a "rut" to become a religious "nut."

Be careful not to be set in your ways, or you may get in God's way. When we come as a child, we can walk in true freedom and be holy instead of holey:

> *But as he which hath called you is holy, so be ye holy in all manner of conversation; because it is written, Be ye holy; for I am holy.*   1 Peter 1:15-16

God must have a holy people, for He is holy, and the thing that keeps us from being holy is our holey soul. A holey soul cannot contain the blessings of God. In this passage of scripture, we see that even our conversation is to be holy. Why are our conversations not holy? Conversations are confirmations of the inner man. Because our soul is full of holes, we speak what is in our hearts:

> *A good man out of the good treasure of his heart bringeth forth that which is good; and an evil man out of the evil treasure of his heart bringeth forth that which is evil: for of the abundance of the heart his mouth speaketh.*   Luke 6:45

Before the Fall, Adam and Eve only heard one way, and that way was good. They did not know evil, so everything they heard was good. Wouldn't it be heavenly to only hear good things? Evil made us double-minded. Therefore, we have become dull of hearing since the Fall. Adam and Eve became DULL because they were no longer FULL! If we desire to be made whole, we must be able to hear the good so that the good can overcome the evil. Evil spelled backward is live. Evil in-a-me is any way I am not living a whole life.

The Bible is full of scriptures concerning the importance of hearing:

He that hath ears to hear, let him hear.

Matthew 11:15

He that hath an ear, let him hear what the Spirit saith unto the churches; To him that overcometh will I give to eat of the tree of life, which is in the midst of the paradise of God.   **Revelation 2:7**

He that hath an ear, let him hear what the Spirit saith unto the churches; To him that overcometh will I give to eat of the hidden manna, and will give him a white stone, and in the stone a new name written, which no man knoweth saving he that receiveth it.   **Revelation 2:17**

He that hath an ear, let him hear what the Spirit saith unto the churches.   **Revelation 3:13**

Adam and Eve would now hear two ways and see two ways, because sin brought forth a division. The heart came about because the soul and spirit would now be housed in a body. Adam's heart would be joined to Eve's heart, and the two would become one:

> *Therefore shall a man leave his father and his mother, and shall cleave unto his wife: and they shall be one flesh.* Genesis 2:24

This is why a man and his wife become one in holy matrimony, because it would now take two halves to make a whole. Sin separated Adam and Eve from the Father. Instead of being one with God, they were divided and became one with each other. Can you visualize two ears coming together to make one:

The heart houses the spirt and the soul, and as a result, our mouths speak what is in our hearts. Unfortunately, most of what we say is half the truth. Notice the words *ear* and *earth* in the word *heart*. The serpent beguiled Eve with his words (tongue), and the words went into her ears and caused division. The Word of God speaks a lot about the waywardness of the tongue. The serpent's tongue became divided as he brought forth division among God's children. Double hearing and double seeing came into play at this time, and we have been double-minded ever since.

The tongue is the hardest thing in our lives to bridle because it is influenced by the soul:

> *Even so the tongue is a little member, and boasteth*
> *great things. Behold, how great a matter a little fire*
> *kindleth!*   James 3:5

As a matter of fact, the tongue has the ability to speak life or death:

> *Death and life are in the power of the tongue: and*
> *they that love it shall eat the fruit thereof.*
>   Proverbs 18:21

It is the tongue that produces the fruit. Be careful not to use your tongue for double-minded conversations, or you may wake up with a split tongue instead of a whole tongue!

Wholeness must come to our souls in order for the holiness of God to fill us, seal us, and heal us from all of the negative, painful issues that we experience in life. The reason we are not seeing any more healings than we are is because our holey souls cannot contain or receive the holiness that God pours into them. God's presence is His holiness.

Imagine being thirsty after working in the sun for hours and finally getting to take a break to get something cool to drink. If your cup is full of holes, it cannot contain the water that is poured into it. You are only able to drink the water that seeps from the holes. Therefore, your thirst is not quenched. No longer are you only hot and thirsty, but you are also exhausted from trying to catch the water that is seeping out. It is impossible to be filled from a cup with holes in it? You can only get a taste of the water, but you cannot get filled. Frustration comes as you catch the water flowing out of the holes. The water runs out before your thirst is satisfied.

Does this sound like a description of your condition? The same is true with our souls. God pours forth His presence to fill our souls, only for us to drink what we can from what seeps out of our holey souls. This is what happens in a good church service. We get a taste of God. But holey is not HOLY.

Think it not strange that this was the first complaint the Israelites had when God delivered them from Egypt:

> *And there was no water for the congregation: and they gathered themselves together against Moses and against Aaron.* Numbers 20:2

They would not get their soul holes healed. Therefore, they died in the wilderness (a dry place). As human beings, thirst is one thing that we all have to contend with. The living waters of God's glory is what we are truly thirsting for. We need to be a fountain springing up, not a holey, leaking vessel that can't be filled.

LIVING WATER FOR YOUR SOUL

Apparently, the Samaritan woman was able to get her soul holes filled with living water before she ran to share her experience with others. This filling filled the soul holes she had suffered from the fear, rejection, and abandonment that had come from the traumas of her many failed relationships. Failed relationships are the evidence of underdeveloped indented emotions (soul holes) that are trying to find a place of completion.

Our soul recognizes the danger of soul holes and tries to close to correct the problem. Unfortunately, when our soul closes, it disables us from our deliverance. Our soul forms holes because of the pain we experience. We associate emptiness with the pain. As a consequence, the soul holes grow ever larger because we shut down emotionally to never feel that pain again.

These soul holes cause us to reject ourselves—and everyone else. The truth is that as we emotionally shut down, we begin the process of withering physically, mentally, and emotionally. We are in control, and we promise ourselves that we will never be hurt that way again.

Soul holes project to us lies that keep us from developing mature and healthy relationships. Some people only love others from a distance, as this lessens their chances of getting hurt. The living water (glory) is the truth that desires to fill in your valleys, bring down your mountaintops, and make your crooked places straight.

Water (glory) is the only solution capable of fulfilling this passage of scripture. We must allow the truth to fill in our soul holes, and as it fills the holes, we will be made whole ourselves. Then it will be possible for us to minister to others. As we make ourselves available to receive the knowledge concerning our soul holes, and we learn how to get them filled, then we can become holy.

The presence of God is holy. Therefore, when we get our soul holes filled to the point that we can contain God's presence, we can become holy.

God desires that our spirit, body, and soul be made whole. How do we get the holes in our souls filled? We first need to come to the realization that traumas, painful experiences, and life in general have created holes in our souls. Life is full of situations that cause soul holes. Some people just live their lives with interrupted, indented souls. They have no goal of being made whole. I think that it would be fair to say that most people do not know they have soul holes.

I wouldn't have known about soul holes either if I hadn't been desperately seeking my healing. I was so desperate for the truth that God gave me this insight into soul holes, so that I could be free and be able to help others get free. You must hunger and thirst in order to be filled. The Lord says that you are blessed if you hunger and thirst after righteousness:

> *Blessed are those who hunger and thirst for righteousness for they shall be filled.* Matthew 5:6

Blessed in this passage of scripture means being filled. When you are full, you can be thank-FULL. Glory to God!

YOU MUST HUNGER AND THIRST
TO BE FILLED!

What needs filled? Surely not your belly! Fill your soul holes in order to be made whole. Many use addictive substances in an effort to fill their soul holes, when only God's Spirit can do it. When God gets enough of His children filled with His glory, then His Kingdom can come, and His will can be done on Earth as it is in Heaven.

We need to come out of agreement with the common thought: "This is the way my life is, and I have to live this way." The truth is the only thing that will set us free. The truth cannot set us free if we cannot contain it in our souls because of the holes.

When we have soul holes, we hear the truth, and then it seeps through our souls and out through the soul holes. I am reminded of a cartoon that I watched when I was young about a cowboy who got shot. He didn't know that he had gotten shot until he drank some water, and it came out of the bullet holes. As human beings, we get shot with bullets of offences, rejections, and fears. We don't realize that we have been hit until the living waters leak out of us, causing a puddle of emotions and pain.

We know the truth, but it cannot set us free because our souls cannot contain the glory that it takes to change us:

77

> *But we all, with open face beholding as in a glass the glory of the Lord, are changed into the same image from glory to glory, even as by the Spirit of the Lord.*   2 Corinthians 3:18

Soul holes are indentions in the soul that have been formed due to painful experiences. The indentions (holes) can only be filled by the glory of God. The glory is the only thing that can change us. Therefore, because our soul holes have a voice, they will tell us the opposite of God's truth. God knows that if we could have changed ourselves, we would have done so already.

We acknowledge wholeness through the daily reading of God's Word. Unfortunately, after a few days, we find ourselves back involved with the things we desired to be free from. Because of the soul holes, we cannot contain what the Word deposits within us, and the outcome is discouraging.

Paul even struggled with this same issue and, therefore, said it best:

> *For that which I do I allow not: for what I would, that do I not; but what I hate, that do I.*   Romans 7:15

I will give you a simple South Georgia translation for this scripture: "Why is it that I do the things I don't need to do, and the things I need to do never get done?"

CONSIDER YOUR WAYS
Maybe we need to consider our ways:

*Now therefore thus saith the L*ord *of hosts; Consider your ways. Ye have sown much, and bring in little; ye eat, but ye have not enough; ye drink, but ye are not filled with drink; ye clothe you, but there is none warm; and he that earneth wages earneth wages to put it into a bag with holes.*   Haggai 1:5-6

In this passage of scripture, the *bag with holes* describes our holey souls. We journey through life overcoming many obstacles, but are ostracized by few obstacles we can't overcome. These obstacles are due to soul holes. We need to realize that the undealt-with issues which we stuffed down deep within our souls are still there. Buried emotions never die.

Our personalities become compromised because we have not had the knowledge of the glory to reveal our soul holes. Therefore, we don't know how to get our soul holes filled. Each morning, when we get up, we hope our day will change, but the truth is that your day is waiting for *you* to change. Hopefully, after reading this book, you will have a clear understanding of what soul holes are and how to get them healed.

We must consider our ways. Many times, we do things out of our brokenness, and then we wonder why life deals us such a bad hand. We have been so broken that we have automatically assumed that the way we do things is the best way. Not so! Consider your ways. They may not be the ways in which you should conduct yourself. If your life is not working for you or for others, you might not be going about it the right way.

I have people tell me, "This is just the way I am." Well, how's that working for you? Or, better yet, how's that working for your children, your co-workers, your neighbors, or your spouse? Would it be so hard for you to consider considering your ways?

By the way, your own way is considered vainglory. Try it and see what happens. The outcome could very well be the change you have been looking for. We may not be aware of our wrongs, because we have defended our soul holes for so long. There are many different ways that our souls become full of holes. Therefore, we must understand where they came in, as we seek God's help in getting set free from them.

BURIED EMOTIONS NEVER DIE!

We see another analogy of soul holes in the following passage of scripture that warns us against putting new wine into old wine skins:

> *And no man putteth new wine into old bottles: else the new wine doth burst the bottles, and the wine is spilled, and the bottles will be marred: but new wine must be put into new bottles.*   Mark 2:22

The new bottles represent a soul without holes. Let's take another look at another scripture that confirms the importance of letting the old go in order to make room for the new:

> *No man putteth a piece of new cloth unto an old garment, for that which is put in to fill it up taketh from the garment, and the rent is made worse.*
>
> Matthew 9:16

Soul holes represent the old wounds that are still prevalent within our souls and disable us from containing the glory that God desires to pour forth upon us. God cannot do a new thing within us unless we are willing to let go of the old. Repentance is the pathway on which we must travel if we are to arrive at our destiny.

Dear Heavenly Father,

I purpose and choose with my free will to repent for any and all ways that I have ignored Your insights into my original afflictions. I desire to consider my ways, that I may be set free and renewed to carry Your glory. Show me Your glory so that I may know the obstacles that have overcome me the majority of my life.

In Jesus' name!

In order for us to be made whole, we must seek the truth. The Word of God says that the only thing that can set us free is truth:

Then said Jesus to those Jews which believed on him, If ye continue in my word, then are ye my disciples indeed; and ye shall know the truth, and the truth shall make you free. John 8:31-32

The holes that lie deep within our souls, are an attempt to keep us from being set free. These holes are formed from lies that keep us from the truth. Soul holes hate truth. When you begin to get set free, don't be surprised if your soul holes act up. We must learn how to apply the truth to the lies and come out of agreement with the very things that will bring us destruction. If the only thing that can set me free is the truth, then I must take that truth and apply it to my individual soul holes. In other words, each soul hole has to be identified before the truth can be applied.

We will be talking about the many different types of soul holes and how to identify them. They are enemies of a whole soul. How do I become holy when I am so full of soul holes?

1. IDENTIFY YOUR SOUL HOLES
2. COME OUT OF THE DENIAL OF UNDEALT-WITH ISSUES AND EMOTIONS
3. HUMBLE YOURSELF, REPENT, AND ASK THE LORD TO FILL YOU WITH HIS GLORY

WARNING: In order for a person to be filled, he or she must have the knowledge of the glory of God. The lack of knowledge of God's glory will leave one empty and full of soul holes.

82

CHAPTER 3

IDENTIFYING YOUR SOUL HOLES

Before I formed thee in the belly I knew thee; and before thou camest forth out of the womb I sanctified thee, and I ordained thee a prophet unto the nations.   Jeremiah 1:5

Identification is the revelation of your indentions. Identification is also the key ingredient to walking in authority. If you do not know who you are, then you do not know how to fulfill your destiny. The reason we are on earth is to fulfill the mission of the Great Commission. Your destiny outcome is directed by your soul choices. If your soul has too many holes, then you will never fulfill your destiny. Most Christians do not even know what their destiny is, much less how to fulfill it.

When counseling, the number one question I ask people is, "Why do you do the things you do not want to do?" The usual response is, "I don't know." The reason we don't know is because soul holes have stolen our identities. We do things that we know we shouldn't do, and then the guilt and shame come to ensure that we never get our souls healed.

Soul holes will not only steal your identity; they will also steal your destiny. Your true identity is your destiny. The word *DENT* is in iDENTity. A soul hole is an inDENTion of the soul caused by painful experiences. If you succumb to a traumatic indention, you will not have a true identity intention.

Many people wonder around their whole lives (like the Israelites in the wilderness), searching for purpose in life. You are the purpose in your life. You are your destiny. The real reasons we are here on this earth is to identify with ourselves, God, and others. Soul holes make you doubt your identity, question God, and reject others.

You can have soul holes that tell you, "You are not worthy!" You can also have soul holes that tell you how much you deserve, and that *other people owe you.* Soul holes cannot tell the truth, so be careful when you are influenced by them. We must get to the place where we can discern our own souls. Be careful not to fall into your soul holes as you get close enough to discern them.

This can be challenging. When you get close to identifying the soul hole, you will also feel the emotion that has tormented you from the emotional indention. *Feel* is the counterfeit to *fill*. If you are under the undue pressure of your feelings, you will not be able to be filled.

The feeling of a tooth will send you to the dentist to get the tooth filled. The purpose of pain is to find the root of the untruth that caused the insanity. What do I mean by that? Have you ever acted in a way that was insane, and later it was hard to believe that you even acted in that way? This is due to your soul holes. A person who flies off the handle has a soul hole of anger. A person who always plays the victim has a soul hole of victimization. A person who always talks of themselves may have a soul hole of self-exaltation and pride. The intent of a soul hole is to make you fall short of God's glory.

Think about walking on a road and suddenly you fall in a hole. The hole represents your soul hole, and the road represents your life. The hole can cause you to fall.

Pain comes as a result of the fall, and instability follows. If the earth is going to be filled with God's glory, then we must get over our muddy emotions. These emotions are the reason you feel like you have been drug through the mud. God's glory is represented by water. May the glory cleanse you of all the muddy emotions that have caused you to feel filthy. May the glory of God fill your soul holes as the mountains are being brought down, valleys filled, and the crooked places made straight:

> *Every valley shall be filled, and every mountain and hill shall be brought low; and the crooked shall be made straight, and the rough ways shall be made smooth.* Luke 3:5

True discernment starts with your own soul. God desires for us to humble ourselves, not think too much or too little of ourselves. His truth offers us perfect balance and is the only thing that will set us free.

Now that we know that soul holes not only interrupt our souls, but also interrupt our destiny, we can now identify what has assaulted our identities. The law states that we are innocent until proven guilty.

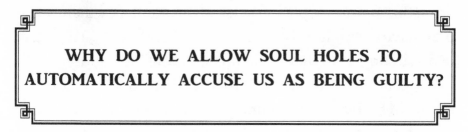

WHY DO WE ALLOW SOUL HOLES TO AUTOMATICALLY ACCUSE US AS BEING GUILTY?

This is the first step in the process of getting set free from our many soul holes. The question is not if you have soul holes. If you have a soul, you have soul holes. Most people do not know about soul holes, but that doesn't mean they're not there. It may be that you know there is more of God you desire to experience, but you don't know how to get to the *more*. This is because your soul holes have kept you from experiencing the *more* of God.

To receive the *more* of God, you must make room in your soul. Fear, rejection, and abandonment have occupied a large percentage of our souls and have left only a small portion available for obedience and change. *Hole* is the counterfeit to *whole*. If you desire to be whole, then you will have to evict the soul holes and make room for God's wholeness to come to your soul. Wherever a soul hole remains, the presence of God is restrained.

The larger the soul hole, the greater the damage. Soul holes can come in different sizes, much like your morning coffee at a Quick Stop. We will eventually learn how to get our large soul holes filled, and when we do, the medium and small ones will have to go as well. Until we master getting the large ones filled, we will work on whichever smaller ones come up first.

Remember, this is a process, and we must try not to get too impatient with ourselves. It took our whole lives to acquire all these holes. Therefore, we will have to go back through the holes to become whole.

One may say, "I don't believe that you have to go back through the pain to be set free." The truth is that you will inevitably continue to go through the pain unless you do go back through the soul holes to be made whole.

Think about entering a room that has only one door and no windows. In order to come out of that room, you must exit where you entered. The same is true with soul holes. We must go back to their origin to exit the pain. You must face it to erase it. The only way to be set free is to open the places you have closed due to the pain and torment of the soul hole. Then you must apply the truth to the hole and ask God to fill the hole with His presence (glory).

To be filled with God's glory, you must first know what His glory is. God introduced me to His glory 3,944 days ago, and since then my life has never been the same.[5] I started walking in my destiny the day God introduced me to His glory. It is the glory of God that we need in our lives to make us whole:

I will go before thee, and make the crooked places straight: I will break in pieces the gates of brass,

5. I wrote about my glory experience in my first book, **The Well of God's Glory Unveiled.**

and cut in sunder the bars of iron: And I will give thee the treasures of darkness, and hidden riches of secret places, that thou mayest know that I, the Lord, which call thee by thy name, am the God of Israel. Isaiah 45:2-3

Remember the story of Moses at the burning bush? On that day, Moses was introduced to God's glory, which introduced him to his destiny. You must know the glory of God if you are to walk in your destiny. When the glory parted the sea for Moses, it was an illustration of Moses' ways versus (vs.) God's ways. It makes you wonder why we call scriptures verses (mankind's way vs. God's way). We say that we desire God's ways, but we end up taking our own route of doubt.

God's ways are much higher than our ways, but we must have the glory of God to separate us from the old for us to walk in the new. The glory of God brought great adventures for Moses as he overcame his fear to draw near to God:

But lift thou up thy rod, and stretch out thine hand over the sea, and divide it: and the children of Israel shall go on dry ground through the midst of the sea. Exodus 14:16

God always provides a way out for those who believe. This dry ground is a supernatural passageway for the impossible to be possible. This is an example of how we are supposed to cross over on dry ground, not get stuck. However, if you don't move when God moves, you could drown.

The soul holes in our soul have the ability to drown us with negative emotions. Soul holes are the dry places of our souls that we have not allowed God to saturate. These dry places will never be saturated and filled unless we allow the truth of God to flood in and relieve us of our spiritual dehydration. We relive what is not relieved.

The Bible describes these dry places in Matthew 12:43-45:

> *When the unclean spirit is gone out of a man, he walketh through dry places, seeking rest, and findeth none. Then he saith, I will return into my house from whence I came out; and when he is come, he findeth it empty, swept, and garnished. Then goeth he, and taketh with himself seven other spirits more wicked than himself, and they enter in and dwell there: and the last state of that man is worse than the first. Even so shall it be also unto this wicked generation.*

Here, God is giving us examples of soul holes that house spirits such as fear, rejection, and abandonment—just to name a few. When we allow these negative emotions to abide and hide, we remain incarcerated in our own conditions. If we are not careful, the soul holes become such a part of us that we have a hard time discerning the truth. If it is not whole, it is not the truth. Too many times, we, as Christians, defend our brokenness. Why? Because we have lived so long with our soul holes that brokenness feels like part of who we are. Once you defend your brokenness, the soul hole has the potential to double in size.

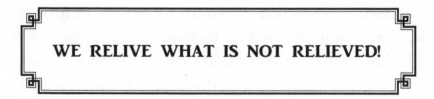

WE RELIVE WHAT IS NOT RELIEVED!

Once we identify a soul hole, come out of denial, and re-pent, then the soul hole can be filled with God's glory. Once the soul hole is filled, the unclean spirit can still return with seven times the power to see if we are truly healed. If we do not keep our temple swept and clean, the unclean spirits can come back in, and our latter state will be worse than our former state.

God gives us authority to cast out unclean spirits, but the problem is: we cast them out of other people and not out of ourselves:

> *And he ordained twelve, that they should be with him, and that he might send them forth to preach, and to have power to heal sicknesses, and to cast out devils.*   Mark 3:14-15

You have the power to cast devils out of other people, but God has given you the power to first cast them out of your-self. Many Christians do not believe they can have unclean spirits. This is a no brainer! If you don't think you can have an unclean spirit, then you will never cast it out.

By the way, unclean spirits that dwell in soul holes invite afflictions to come into the body.

SOUL HOLES ARE DRY PLACES WHERE SPIRITS CAN DWELL!

In other words, you may be trying to cast out cancer, when the culprit is the soul hole that houses the cancer. Shut down the soul hole, and the cancer will have to flee.

I once knew a lady who was a caregiver for her friend, who had lung cancer. Sadly, her friend succumbed to a pre-mature death. Six-months after her friend died, the caregiver fell sick and received a diagnosis of lung cancer. She had a fear of cancer soul hole, and she developed lung cancer. If this woman had identified the soul hole, come out of agreement with it, and repented, she could have been set free. Unfortunately, she also succumbed to a pre-mature death.

Another example is praying against a heart attack but not attending to the soul hole of a broken heart. Soul holes are the culprits that house the afflictions. It is important that we know the glory of God because the glory of God brings us revelation to reveal hidden mysteries. The hidden mystery could be the insight into the affliction that could bring one's healing.

I love the story of Jesus telling Peter to cast his net on the other side of the boat. Peter had fished all night and caught naught. Then, suddenly, Jesus appeared and told him to cast the net on the other side, where he caught a draught:

Now when he had left speaking, he said unto Simon, Launch out into the deep, and let down your nets for a draught. And Simon answering said unto him, Master, we have toiled all the night, and have taken nothing: nevertheless, at thy word I will let down the net. And when they had this done, they enclosed a great multitude of fishes: and their net brake. And they beckoned unto their partners, which were in the other ship, that they should come and help them. And they came, and filled both the ships, so that they began to sink. When Simon Peter saw it, he fell down at Jesus' knees, saying, Depart from me; for I am a sinful man, O Lord. For he was astonished, and all that were with him, at the draught of the fishes which they had taken.   Luke 5:4-9

Sometimes, we need to cast our nets on the other side if we are to see a miracle. When we do all that we know to do, it is apparent that we need to be willing to try a different way. If you want a different result, you must do something different.

Jesus' presence brought forth the insight that revealed the hidden mystery. The hidden mystery revealed was that the fish were on the other side from where Peter was fishing. Try casting on the other side, and see what you catch. Things are not always as they seem. Jesus has a way of showing us that our answers are on the other side of our ritualistic ways.

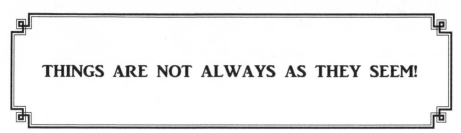

THINGS ARE NOT ALWAYS AS THEY SEEM!

I have a friend who is a whiz at untangling necklaces. I have no patience when it comes to tangled necklaces. In fact, I have been known to just give up and throw them in the trash. My friend taught me to always start the untangling process in the center of the knot. When you can find the tightest part of the knot and loosen it, then the knot must come apart.

We must go to the center of our soul hole (knot) if we are to bring relief to the place in our soul that has the greatest entanglement. As we disentangle the knot (things that are NOT supposed to be there), we will begin to get relief. We can no longer afford to throw valuable relationships away just because our soul holes cause knots (relationships NOT to happen). When one of our soul holes collides with another person's soul hole, the end result is "rejecterous"! Of course, I made that word up.

LIVE VS. EVIL

Part of the process is this: You will have to identify the hole as a soul hole (a place in need of a healing), come out of agreement with it, repent, and then allow the truth to set you free. It doesn't always work on the first attempt. The depth of your soul hole and how long you have had it will be the deciding factors in the outcome. But, rest assured, those who seek shall find:

> *Ask, and it shall be given you; seek, and ye shall find; knock, and it shall be opened unto you.*
>
> Matthew 7:7

I would like to share with you the insight God gave me concerning identifying soul holes. God will use analogies, or parables, to get us to see things differently. When someone asks me a question I don't understand, I will ask them to rearrange the words and ask me again. Why? I have dyslexia and, therefore, I see differently than others. Usually, if the words are rearranged, asking the same question, then I can answer the question.

Sometimes, God has to rearrange things, such as in parables, to get us to understand differently than we currently see. Or, in my case, to see differently in order to understand. Being dyslexic has helped me to understand God because I see backwards compared to how normal people see.

For example: Whereas most people see the word *live*, I see it as *evil*. Whereas most people see the word *devil*, I see it as *lived*. *Emordnilap* is a word that means "a description of a word spelled backward." *Palindrome* is a word that means "a phrase that reads the same whether you spell it forward or backward." Examples are *madam, solos, level, mom, dad,* and *wow. Palindrome* spelled backward is *emordnilap*.

For many years, I thought I was strange. It wasn't until I embraced my *odd* that I found that it was *God*. I quit rejecting what was different in me, embraced it, and found the hidden mysteries of my soul. I don't have a disability; I have a supernatural ability to see things the opposite of others, and this brings forth revelation to reverse the curse.

Now let's get back to the parable God revealed to me?

If you have a fruit tree and notice that the fruit is diseased, the disease usually does not start in the fruit. Identifying fruit tree disease requires careful observation of the different stages of the tree throughout the seasons. First, you must keep a record of the growth and blossoming. Reduced growth is a sure sign of disease.

We need to understand that disease is not only what a doctor diagnoses. Disease is anyway that your soul is at "dis-ease." "Dis ease" is the taking away of ease. Guilt and shame are a "dis-ease" of your soul. Understand that I am not only describing a fruit tree; I may be describing your life.

First, we must take accountability and observe the reason why we are not growing and blossoming. Second, we need to check on the leaves. Have you ever thought about how much humans are like trees? Humans have taste <u>buds</u>, grow <u>limbs</u>, and <u>leaves</u> when they get mad. The Word of God even talks about this bizarre parallel:

> *And he shall be like a tree planted by the rivers of water, that bringeth forth his fruit in his season; his leaf also shall not wither; and whatsoever he doeth shall prosper.*   Psalm 1:3

We must analyze our issues of rejection and abandonment and find a solution as to why we *leave* ourselves and others when we experience rejection and pain. The truth is that we try to protect our loved ones from their pain because we do not want to hurt them. Often, the very opposite takes place, and because of our pain, we walk away from those we love. Hurt people hurt people.

Is there someone you have walked away from? Start identifying your soul hole of rejection, come out of denial, repent, and ask God to fill your soul hole of rejection with His glory.

We are the world's worst if we don't want to deal with something or someone and just close down and leave. Real Christians deal with identifying their soul holes, so that they can be made whole. If we close up, we will never be made whole. If we don't live, we do the opposite. *Live* spelled backward is *evil*. Choose this day whom you will serve—live or evil. Live, don't leave!

> **And if it seem evil unto you to serve the LORD, choose you this day whom ye will serve; whether the gods which your fathers served that were on the other side of the flood, or the gods of the Amorites, in whose land ye dwell: but as for me and my house, we will serve the LORD.** Joshua 24:15

Usually, if disease is present, the leaves of a tree will curl up around the edges or become discolored. Some leaves shrivel up and become disfigured. Does this sound familiar?

Repeat each letter of the word *close* out loud—C L O S E. What does this spell? If you said *close* (the opposite of open), then this is the state of your soul. If you said *close* (nearness to something) then you have been prepared to go ahead and get your soul set free. Both words are spelled the same, but most people are more familiar with closing down than being intimately close with others. As humans, we tend to close when we experience "dis-ease," and the result is detrimental to our mental, physical, and spiritual health.

Lastly, the bark, which is the outer covering of the tree, needs to be inspected. Discoloration, spots, or cankers may appear on the bark because of internal distress. Some cankers will even form tumors that begin to seep a dark gum-like substance (this may explain the cancer epidemic in believers).

In essence, the fruit is the evidence of the fruit tree's existence. We are like fruit trees, as we are trying to survive the seasons of life with vigilance and longevity. We produce good fruit as a result of our efforts:

> *For a good tree bringeth not forth corrupt fruit; neither doth a corrupt tree bring forth good fruit. For every tree is known by his own fruit. For of thorns men do not gather figs, nor of a bramble bush gather they grapes.*　　　　Luke 6:43-44

The fruit is usually the last part of the tree to experience "disease." We must go deep within the tree, even into the root system, if we desire to get to the origin of the dis-ease. The roots are where the truth lies:

> *And there shall come forth a rod out of the stem of Jesse, and a Branch shall grow out of his roots: And the spirit of the LORD shall rest upon him, the spirit of wisdom and understanding, the spirit of counsel and might, the spirit of knowledge and of the fear of the LORD; and shall make him of quick understanding in the fear of the LORD: and he shall not judge after the sight of his eyes, neither reprove after the hearing of his ears: but with righteousness*

shall he judge the poor, and reprove with equity for the meek of the earth: and he shall smite the earth: with the rod of his mouth, and with the breath of his lips shall he slay the wicked. And righteousness shall be the girdle of his loins, and faithfulness the girdle of his reins. Isaiah 11:1-5

If our fruit is bad, it is because evil has taunted the roots that keep us from producing live fruit. We cannot bear good fruit if we have "dis-ease" in our roots. When we get to the bottom of our soul holes, then we can deal with the root issues of our lives and become whole.

THE IDENTITY DIS-EASE

The number one reason we do not deal with our issues is because of our lack of knowledge:

My people are destroyed for lack of knowledge: because thou hast rejected knowledge, I will also reject thee, that thou shalt be no priest to me: seeing thou hast forgotten the law of thy God, I will also forget thy children. Hosea 4:6

Even though we can "quote the Heaven" out of some scriptures, we have not been taught how to deal with our soul issues. We have learned how to memorize the Word in order to get a gold star, but we have no clue as to how to receive deep insight and revelation concerning our own issues.

God is not looking for a star; He desires for us to know who we truly are. We don't understand why we do the things we do. The truth is that our soul holes coerce us to do and say things we would not normally say and do. Think about that certain situation you reacted to out of your soul hole, and you "showed your tail." Showing your tail is not the answer; the answer is that we need the truth to get our soul holes healed. As a matter of fact, when we act like a tail, it is because the lie (tale) is trying to exist. We are to be the head and not the tail:

> *And the LORD shall make thee the head, and not the tail; and thou shalt be above only, and thou shalt not be beneath; if that thou hearken unto the commandments of the LORD thy God, which I command thee this day, to observe and to do them.*
>
> Deuteronomy 28:13

Soul holes cause us to make a "tail" out of ourselves because our head (mind) knows better. Usually, after a person shows out, he or she will be sorry and say, "I knew better than that." Our soul holes cause us to say things that we later regret, but it is in us, or we wouldn't have said it in the first place.

We fear that we will not be able to get rid of what we do not understand. The lack of knowledge will keep you stuck in the insanities of your own mind. We know how we should feel, but many times we feel the opposite, and we end up discouraged by the fact that this may be a permanent reality. Our soul holes will not allow us to be filled, and that is why we get stuck in our feelings.

Feelings are the counterfeit to *fillings*. A hole must be filled for it to no longer be identified as a hole. Are you in a hole, or are you whole? A hole becomes whole only when it gets filled with the glory (truth).

If your soul hole can distract you with a feeling, then your soul hole cannot be filled. The evidence of our soul holes being filled is that we operate as the head and not the tail.

Have you ever heard the phrase, *no strings attached?* Well, there are many strings attached when it comes to dealing with soul holes. Every hole has a string that is attached (literally) to an emotion. When there are many holes and strings, things become twisted, tangled, and detrimental. The soul hole lies and tries to line up with other people's soul holes, thus causing more pain.

Soul holes desire to identify with other soul holes, so they can connect and cause double the pain. Beware: your soul holes crave being filled by other soul holes. In other words, you will be attracted to whomever has the same soul holes as you do.

Eve ate half of the fruit and gave Adam the other half, and that made him her other half. For far too long, we have been seeking others to make us whole, when God is the only one who can do that for you. A husband or wife cannot make you whole. But, if you get your soul holes filled, you will make a better wife or husband.

We form relationships out of a foundation of "holey-ness," and we line our soul holes up with other people's soul holes. This causes an entangled web of emotions that make more soul holes.

While counseling one of my children before she walked down the aisle in marriage, I encouraged her to get her soul holes healed before she became one with another. Unfortunately, her soul holes plus his soul holes made one big hole, and they both fell into it. This puts a new perspective on the phrase *falling in love*. The truth is the only answer to untangling all the soul hole lies"

> *Stand fast therefore in the liberty wherewith Christ hath made us free, and be not entangled again with the yoke of bondage.* Galatians 5:1

Soul holes are like scar tissue that grows because of traumatic damage. In time, if not dealt with, the scar tissue will cause more damage than the original wound. The wound was a contact point of interruption, and the scar tissue continues to cause damage to the place that was interrupted. The wound represents the soul hole, and the scar tissue that continues to grow represents the strings that attach themselves to other people's issues.

If we are not careful, we, like Moses, can spend a lifetime taking care of someone else's business. Your soul holes will get entangled with the soul holes of others, and then you will wind up dramatically involved.

Moses was desperate when he found the glory on the backside of Mt. Horeb. *Horeb* means "desolation." Moses was desperate to get his soul holes healed. Therefore, he turned to inquire of the glory, he encountered the glory, and his soul holes began to heal. Then, he could complete his commission.

We must take accountability, identify the scar tissue issue, and get healed of any reoccurring conditions:

The thief cometh not, but for to steal, and to kill, and to destroy: I am come that they might have life, and that they might have it more abundantly.

John 10:10

The scar tissue will entangle itself around ligaments, tendons, and organs in search of a place to reside. Many times, our soul holes will seek a place to connect to another's soul holes, to find companionship. Misery loves company! Again, this is a place where the lack of knowledge can destroy you. The destruction is intended for your children, but first it has to influence you to get to them. It is time to rise up, identify every false thought within our souls, and be made whole.

Once identified, the soul holes can now be relieved (through repentance) of the guilt and shame of acting certain ways that are not pleasing to God, to you, and to others. You will be amazed when you finally get free of the soul holes that have kept you in bondage for years. Suddenly, you will not react the way you have always reacted, and then you will know that the truth has filled your soul holes.

Don't stop when you start getting relief because there are many more soul holes that need to be filled and healed. The healing only comes after the filling.

To be filled one must hunger and thirst after righteousness. Soul holes have a way of influencing your fears, encouraging your insecurities, and compromising your completeness. To identify soul holes, we must define the culprit of confusion.

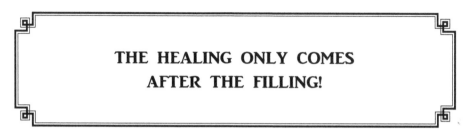

THE HEALING ONLY COMES
AFTER THE FILLING!

SOUL TIES

The next issue at hand is "soul ties." Soul ties can be formed from relationships that have been established while under the influence of soul holes (Relationships Under the Influence). We have had many RUI's in our lives that have caused us to crash. It is time to sober up and face our soul holes that have intoxicated us with lies.

Soul holes led us to soul ties. God desires to intoxicate us with His true intimacy, but soul ties prevent us from having true intimacy with God.

Soul ties can come in several different forms. Soul ties are emotional bonds that we form with ourselves and others. Soul ties are not only sexual, but sexual soul ties tend to be the unhealthiest of all. We can form soul ties with co-workers, children, counselors, teachers, and celebrities... And the list goes on.

Infatuation often occurs as the evidence of soul ties:

> *While they promise them liberty, they themselves are the servants of corruption: for of whom a man is overcome, of the same is he brought in bondage.*
>
> 2 Peter 2:19

You are usually a slave to anything that controls you. Jesus was only led by His Father. Soul ties have an emotional, physical, and spiritual hold on all those who get caught up in them anyway you "fictate" in the presence of others. *"Fictate"* is another word I made up. It means "to dictate fiction." Anyway you have to be fake is because of soul holes and soul ties.

Have you ever noticed that people often talk differently around certain other people? This is because they want to impress them, in order to be accepted. When you are involved in a soul tie, other people have the power to distort and control your behavior. To be frankly honest, this is exhausting. You can have a soul tie with whomever you give the permission to captain your character.

Soul ties usually stem from one person needing something from another person to make them feel a certain way. Soul ties do not necessarily require another soul to tie to. Many people have soul ties to gambling, food, drugs, sex, abuse, lying, gossip, alcohol, "drivenness"... and the list goes on and on.

THE ROOT OF MANY SOUL TIES

Many soul ties are formed due to what you did *not* get from your parents and grandparents. I have ministered to many people who were addicted to chemical substance because of not getting nurtured through their mother's breast. They were always seeking someone or something to suck the life out of.

EXAMINE YOURSELF

This would be a great place to stop and ask yourself the question: "Who do I have an unhealthy soul tie with?" Infatuation often occurs as the evidence of soul ties.

THE ROOT OF SEXUAL SOUL TIES

Sexual soul ties come from a need to be loved. Sex is tridimensional—spirit, body, and soul. Therefore, it is much more damaging:

> *Flee fornication. Every sin that a man doeth is without the body; but he that committeth fornication sinneth against his own body.* 1 Corinthians 6:18

Sex outside of holy matrimony brings forth situations beyond humanistic comprehension. There is only one God who can meet the needs of His people, and that is Jehovah-Rapha (the God who heals). No matter how the soul tie is formed, we must be set free from anyone that has an unrighteous, unhealthy amount of influence over us.

It is important to call out the names (even if just in your mind) of the people who you have had sexual relations with. May I lead you in a prayer for you to be released from all soul ties?

Dear Heavenly Father,

I purpose and choose with my free will to repent for any and all unhealthy soul ties in my life. I ask You to forgive me, and I forgive myself. I come out of agreement with all soul ties now and ask that Your truth set me free. I also forgive anyone who has ever influenced me emotionally, spiritually, and/or physically. I come out of agreement with words that have been spoken and deeds that have been done against me, in Jesus' name.

Lord, heal my memory of these things, and annihilate any associations that I have made while under the influence of a soul tie. Holy Spirit, please speak Your words of truth over this situation.

Amen!

WHEN YOU ARE FREE FROM SOUL TIES, YOU ARE FREE INDEED!

LOVE IS THE GREATEST GIFT

Love is the greatest gift because it has the ability to set one free:

> *And now abideth faith, hope, charity, these three; but the greatest of these is charity.*
>
> 1 Corinthians 13:13

Charity is love, and love is to be given freely:

> *Give, and it shall be given unto you; good measure, pressed down, and shaken together, and running*

over, shall men give into your bosom. For with the
same measure that ye mete withal it shall be mea-
sured to you again. Luke 6:38

True love doesn't cost the giver; true love gives without expecting anything in return. If we do not have true love, how can we give what we do not have?

The love that we currently have is the love that has survived legions of fears, regions of rejections, and abandonments of agony. Faith, hope, and love are truths that represent the three-fold cord that is not easily broken. As long as we practice these three things, we will be healed.

There is only one problem: for every ability, there lies lurking in the shadows three disabilities. We must learn how to counteract these disabilities so that we can conquer with the abilities that God has given us. For every good, there is an opposing evil, but with God all things are possible:

But Jesus beheld them, and said unto them, With
men this is impossible; but with God all things are
possible. Matthew 19:26

WE MUST LOVE OURSELVES

The greatest love I have ever experienced has been for my parents and children. It is not hard to love them, but it *is* hard for me to love myself. The Bible says that we are to love others with the same love that we love ourselves:

And the second is like, namely this, Thou shalt love thy neighbour as thyself. There is none other commandment greater than these.   Mark 12:31

Houston, we may have a problem! We haven't been able to love our neighbors because we haven't yet mastered loving ourselves. If we do not love ourselves, we cannot fully operate in the trinity of God. As long as we have soul holes and ties, we will never truly be able to love the way God intended for us to love and be loved.

CREATED TO LOVE AND BE LOVED

Mankind was created to love and be loved. When that love is not satisfied, there will be a need for soul ties. In order to truly love, one must understand the importance of the trinity of God—God the Father, Son and Holy Spirit.

God sent His only begotten Son to die for our sins. This is true love. Jesus laid His life down (voluntarily) because He loves us so much. Furthermore, after the resurrection and ascension of Jesus, God sent His Holy Spirit so that we would not be comfortless.

Everything that we need in life can be found in the trinity of true intimacy. This threefold cord of unity has stood the test of time. The trinity of true intimacy is to LOVE:

1. God
2. Yourself
3. Family and others

We have been guilty of loving our parents and children more than we have loved ourselves. Get your soul holes healed, love yourself for the first time, and see a healing take place in your soul.

PHYSICAL HEALING WILL FOLLOW

When your soul holes get filled, your body will follow:

> *Beloved, I wish above all things that thou mayest prosper and be in health, even as thy soul prospereth.* 3 John 1:2

If you have thought that you couldn't love your children any more than you do, just wait until your soul holes get filled! True intimacy comes forth as the evidence of a healed soul manifests.

We often don't realize how our soul holes have robbed us of our true intimacy with God, others, and ourselves. It is time to get healed and take back everything that has been taken from us and our loved ones.

When we identify our soul holes, then we can come out of agreement with them, and whatever has been stolen from us must be returned seven-fold:

> *But if he be found, he shall restore sevenfold; he shall give all the substance of his house.*
> Proverbs 6:31

1. IDENTIFY YOUR SOUL HOLES
2. COME OUT OF DENIAL OF UNDEALT-WITH ISSUES AND EMOTIONS
3. HUMBLE YOURSELF, REPENT, AND ASK THE LORD TO FILL YOU WITH HIS GLORY

CHAPTER 4

THE THREE-FOLD CORD

And if one prevail against him, two shall withstand him; and a threefold cord is not quickly broken.
                                                                    Ephesians 4:12

The enemy has created a counterfeit to everything God has ever created. If God desires for us to have a whole soul, the enemy desires for us to have holes in our soul. If God says, "LIVE," the enemy says, "EVIL!" *Devil* spelled backwards is *lived*. Our goal is to reverse the curse and receive all that eternity has made possible for this earthen vessel of ours.

Evil is the opposite of the truth, and its purpose is to confuse God's people. God's desire for us is that we are in one accord with Him. Even the light of God's countenance has been imitated by the enemy:

And no marvel; for Satan himself is transformed into an angel of light.   2 Corinthians 11:14

Satan also created a counterfeit of the threefold-cord of unity. The devil's three-fold cord is a three-fold cord of dis-unity. *Disunity* is "a disagreement or conflict within a group." This three-fold cord of disunity is called PRIDE, and it is made up of fear, rejection, and abandonment. If the trinity of true intimacy is faith, hope, and love, then what do you think the enemy would create as a counterfeit three-fold cord? It would be fear, rejection, and abandonment!

This three-fold cord that the enemy created is used to destroy God's children. A good way to discern your spiritual status is to ask yourself, "Am I walking in faith, hope and love or in fear, rejection, and abandonment"? Better yet, ask someone who loves you what you are walking in!

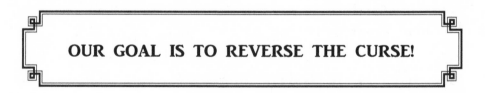

OUR GOAL IS TO REVERSE THE CURSE!

FEAR AS THE ENTRY POINT

Fear is the enemy's entry point. Fear is a seed that grows many other soul holes. While on the subject of fear, let's analyze the different sizes of soul holes? Fear is fear, but it can come in different sizes. For example, the fear of death would be considered a large soul hole. A medium fear soul hole could be the fear of heights. A small fear soul hole could be the fear of a wasp.

Small soul holes are easier to deal with than medium and large soul holes. After a small soul hole is healed, we can come out of denial and allow the truth to set us free from the medium ones and then move on to the larger ones. It is a process, and you must not give up after the small ones are healed. Hopefully, we can get the large fear-of-death soul hole healed so that we won't fall off a high ladder and break our neck because of a wasp sting!

A small soul hole will grow to become larger if not stopped. If the large soul hole, fear of death, is dealt with and healed, then you won't sweat the small stuff. In other words, if the large soul hole, fear of death, is no longer there, then by dealing with the large fear soul hole, you won't have to spend time dealing with the other two. The medium soul hole, fear of heights, along with the small soul hole, fear of wasps, must flee. Remember, the soul holes that you do not deal with will deal with your children and grandchildren.

Panic attacks can be described as extra-large fear soul holes. A childhood friend of mine was deathly afraid of water. He had an extra-large fear soul hole of drowning. Guess what took his life at the young age of sixteen?

> *For the thing which I greatly feared is come upon me, and that which I was afraid of is come unto me. I was not in safety, neither had I rest, neither was I quiet; yet trouble came.* Job 3:25-26

The paramedics told the family that the boy did not die from drowning; he died from his throat constricting. His extra-large fear soul hole caused his throat to close. He was literally scared to death. Do you get the picture?

These are examples of the different sizes of soul holes. If you have panic attacks, you must deal with the extra-large soul hole of fear. When you get the extra-large fear soul hole filled, you will see a big difference in all of your other fears as well. Fear in general, usually grows into other fears.

Fear is a natural emotion, so we all experience it, but we were never intended to get stuck in the rut of fear. A godly fear will keep you from putting your hand to evil. God does not give us evil fear. Therefore, we must overcome fear:

> *For God hath not given us the spirit of fear; but of*
> *power, and of love, and of a sound mind.*
>
> 2 Timothy 1:7

Remember, for every good, there is an evil lurking. Wisdom is identifying the evil, reversing it, and walking in the good. EVIL or LIVE? We must get our fear soul holes filled and healed, or the thing that we fear the most will come upon us.

ONE OF THESE THREE

At times, while going through your process of becoming whole and trying to identify certain soul holes, it may be confusing. Remember that fear, rejection, and abandonment are always the threefold cord to every soul hole. If you don't know what to call your soul hole, it can always be called one of these three.

Now, let's look at the definitions of these three-fold soul holes, and then we will start the process of identifying each one. Understand, that each of these cords has been described here in a limited way.

GODLY THREE-FOLD CORD
FAITH – HOPE – LOVE

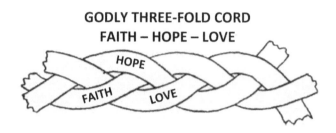

UNGODLY THREE-FOLD CORD
FEAR – REJECTION – ABANDONMENT

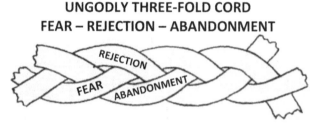

THE FEAR CORD

Fear is an unpleasant, often strong and anxious emotion caused by anticipation or awareness of danger. It is an instinct or awareness of harm in your atmosphere of uncertainty. Fear is a deception formed out of what we have experienced as pain or chaos. It is the first of many soul holes that have been formed to keep you out of true peace.

Fear can come in many forms. One form can be the fear of people and what they may say or do. Other forms can be: fear of being abandoned, fear of being sick, fear of death, fear of the unknown, fear of losing things or people, fear of germs, fear of failure, and on and on.

"The only thing to fear is fear itself" was a quote by Franklin D. Roosevelt during the Second World War. This statement still rings true in the ears of those who are over-coming and identifying soul holes. Fear is a natural emotion; just don't allow it to stay and form other soul holes.

Natural fear is an alarm telling you that something in your atmosphere is wrong. Reverential fear is the beginning of wisdom:

> *The fear of the LORD is the beginning of wisdom,*
> *and the knowledge of the holy is understanding.*
>
> Proverbs 9:10

So, fear is not always a bad thing; it can be a wise thing (if you are in control of it). If, however, we allow fear to stay, then the fear itself can bring forth destruction.

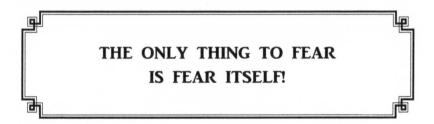

THE ONLY THING TO FEAR IS FEAR ITSELF!

Fear spelled backward is *raef,* which means "kind or com-passionate." One of the variant spellings is *rafe,* which is an English name for a male, meaning "counsel of the wolf" or "wise wolf." *Wolf* spelled backward is *flow.* A wise flow would be opposite of the wolf. If we don't flow with God, then we become wolfish (foolish).

God didn't create mankind as a wolf, but He does use the parallel of a wolf in sheep's clothing. Wolves are the natural

enemies of sheep, and metaphorically speaking, God calls
His people sheep:

> *And when he brings out his own sheep, he goes be-*
> *fore them; and the sheep follow him: for they know*
> *his voice.* John 10:4, NKJV

We need to learn how to flow in the Spirit. Adam met with God
in the cool of the day, and God came up as a mist from the ground:
Before the Fall, Adam and Eve had a reverential fear of
God. Then the big bad wolf (devil) counterfeited their godly
fear with the opposite and caused mankind to hide in fear
of his Creator:

> *And he said, I heard thy voice in the garden, and I*
> *was afraid, because I was naked; and I hid myself.*
> Genesis 3:10

God was the flow from the mist of the garden until that
flow was interrupted by sin. As a remedy for sin, God made
Adam and Eve a covering from the skin of an animal. The
Bible doesn't say what kind of animal it was. It could have
been a sheep. Surely it was not from a wolf. Wolves in the
Bible represent false prophets:

> *Beware of false prophets, which come to you in*
> *sheep's clothing, but inwardly they are ravening*
> *wolves.* Matthew 7:15

117

After the Fall, Adam and Eve left the Garden of Eden and went eastward. Mankind has had to be *right* ever since the Fall because Adam and Eve *left* the garden (a little Eden humor)! If you rearrange the letters in the word Eden, you can spell the word *need*! Adam and Eve became more like the wolf instead of the flow and would need to be needed.

Four river heads began to flow out of the garden, because God's presence was interrupted by the Fall. The rivers began to flow as a result of sin damning up the original flow. Sin brings damnation. Adam and Eve walked away from the flowing presence of God, out into a dry abandoned earth:

> **He that believeth on me, as the scripture hath said,**
> **out of his belly shall flow rivers of living water.**
>
> John 7:38

All rivers lead to the sea. Mankind became the dry and thirsty land that would need the water of God to saturate its soul. God would dwell in the deepest part of man, as he worked out his salvation here on earth.

If *flow* spelled backward is *wolf*, then have we been the wolves in sheep's clothing? Are we the wolf that stopped the flow of God in our life, which is opposite of being the sheep? If this is too deep for you, don't worry about it. Keep flowing!

This is usually how I see things when I receive insight concerning God's original plan (which was turned upside down by man's rebellion). To see the origin of truth revealed, it is wise to reverse what you see in the natural. Too often, we automatically receive what we see in the natural. Can we have faith to see opposite ways, in the hope of seeing the truth of true intimacy revealed?

While we look not at the things which are seen, but at the things which are not seen: for the things which are seen are temporal; but the things which are not seen are eternal. 2 Corinthians 4:18

Do we really trust God, or are we just playing church? In order to overcome the fear soul hole, we must trust God to fill the soul holes in us. I am an ex-drug addict and have been clean for twenty-three years now. My drugs of choice were prescription medications, along with other things that I kept tucked away in zip lock bags. No one knew that I had an addiction because it did not affect me in a negative way. I was able to work and function in my everyday life. I would take pills to go to sleep at night and then take more pills during the day to keep me going. For the most part, I was legal because I had prescriptions for the drugs.

Have you ever wondered why they call it a "pre-scription"? People usually seek medications before they seek the Scriptures. If we would go to the Scriptures first (pre-scriptures), we would see more miraculous healings. I know for a fact that the pharmaceutical companies would not be as prosperous as they are now.

A snake on a rod is the medical symbol for *pharmakeia*, which is the Greek word for pharmacy:

119

And Moses answered and said, But, behold, they will not believe me, nor hearken unto my voice: for they will say, The LORD hath not appeared unto thee. And the LORD said unto him, What is that in thine hand? And he said, A rod. And he said, Cast it on the ground. And he cast it on the ground, and it became a serpent; and Moses fled from before it. And the LORD said unto Moses, Put forth thine hand, and take it by the tail. And he put forth his hand, and caught it, and it became a rod in his hand: That they may believe that the LORD God of their fathers, the God of Abraham, the God of Isaac, and the God of Jacob, hath appeared unto thee. Exodus 4:1-5

When Moses faced Pharaoh and this proud leader rebelled against God, Moses found himself demonstrating signs, wonders, and miracles. A few scriptures down, Moses felt inadequate, so God encouraged him by saying:

And the Lord said unto him, Who hath made man's mouth? or who maketh the dumb, or deaf, or the seeing, or the blind? have not I the LORD? Exodus 4:11

God basically told Moses, "I made man's mouth, and I made some deaf, some dumb and some blind." I don't totally understand all of this, but I do know in some cases that less is more. We won't know everything until we see Jesus face to face. Then we shall be like Him:

> *Beloved, now are we the sons of God, and it doth not yet appear what we shall be: but we know that, when he shall appear, we shall be like him; for we shall see him as he is.*　　　　1 John 3:2

Until then, I am going to keep seeking the truth and allowing it to set me free, so that I can see hidden mysteries revealed.

When hidden mysteries are revealed, it brings forth more understanding as to why things are the way they are. God knows we need more understanding in life. A lack of understanding will keep a man afflicted and addicted, but understanding will grant him access to freedom.

When we can understand, we are able to see and hear differently, and when we can see and hear differently, we can act and react differently. It is dangerous for a man to put his trust in his own understanding, because if he has soul holes, his understanding is incorrect:

> *Trust in the LORD with all thine heart; and lean not unto thine own understanding.*　　　　Proverbs 3:5

> *Wisdom is the principal thing; therefore get wisdom: and with all thy getting get understanding.*
> 　　　　　　　　　　　　　　　　Proverbs 4:7

Understanding will reveal hidden mysteries that God desires to show us so that we can be set free. Here are a few of my favorite hidden mystery scriptures:

Call unto me, and I will answer thee, and show thee great and mighty things, which thou knowest not.
Jeremiah 33:3

He revealeth the deep and secret things: he knoweth what is in the darkness, and the light dwelleth with him.
Daniel 2:22

It is the glory of God to conceal a thing: but the honour of kings is to search out a matter.
Proverbs 25:2

If God can trust you with insight, He will reveal hidden mysteries to you concerning others. He will not give you information about others if you have any hidden agenda and might use the information unrighteously. Hidden mysteries are only revealed as you seek to find them in truth. God will never tell you more than you ask Him for!

When hidden mysteries are revealed, they bring understanding, which will allow you to be able to help others. You will never be able to understand others if you do not understand yourself. When you receive a true understanding of God's Word, then you can truly understand yourself.

God revealed a hidden mystery to me about the life of Moses:

*And Moses said unto the L*ORD*, O my Lord, I am
not eloquent, neither heretofore, nor since thou hast
spoken unto thy servant: but I am slow of speech,
and of a slow tongue.*   Exodus 4:10

Moses had the dumb and deaf spirit. He was *"slow of
speech"* and *"of a slow tongue!"* This is why God sent his
brother, Aaron, with him to confront Pharaoh. Moses was
the one God was speaking about when he said, *"Who has
made man's mouth"* (Exodus 4:11).

God told Moses to throw down his rod. The Bible says
that Moses threw down his rod, it became a serpent, and
Moses fled from it. He was afraid of the snake that the rod
had turned into. He was afraid because he had the dumb
and deaf spirit. He couldn't understand, nor could he communicate what he wanted to say to Pharaoh. This confusion
came in when disobedience dictated destiny.

In Genesis, the serpent beguiled Eve. This was a generational showdown that required the glory of God to reveal the
hidden mysteries that would later set God's chosen people
free. *Evil* created opposition to *live.*

Adam and Eve were as wise as God, but then they ate
the forbidden fruit, which reversed the truth and created
the dumb and deaf. The foundation of the dumb and deaf
spirit is fear! God's anger was kindled against Moses
because the dumb and deaf spirit made Moses think that
he could not do what God had called him to do. Many of
humanities disobedient acts are caused by the dumb and
deaf spirit.

Adam became afraid of God instead of reverentially fearing His Creator. Why was God's anger kindled against Moses? It was because He knew that Moses had the dumb and deaf spirit. He had made Moses free, and now he was in bondage to his fear.

How many times have you feared doing what God called you to do? God made you, so He knows your abilities and disabilities. Disabilities are the opposite of abilities. God is not concerned about your disabilities; He is interested in your availability. Availability to flow in God will reverse your disabilities.

We are still dealing with the dumb and deaf spirit in our lives today as a result of the Fall. The interesting fact about the dumb and deaf spirit is that the disciples could not cast that particular spirit out of the boy in Luke 9:37-42.[6]

THE FOUNDATION OF THE DUMB AND DEAF SPIRIT IS FEAR!

God knew what Moses was facing and allowed his brother, Aaron, to be his mouthpiece:

> *And Moses and Aaron went in unto Pharaoh, and they did so as the LORD had commanded: and Aaron cast down his rod before Pharaoh, and before his servants, and it became a serpent. Then Pharaoh*

6. I write more about this spirit in my pamphlet entitled, **"The Dumb and Deaf Spirit."**

also called the wise men and the sorcerers: now the magicians of Egypt, they also did in like manner with their enchantments. For they cast down every man his rod, and they became serpents: but Aaron's rod swallowed up their rods. And he hardened Pharaoh's heart, that he hearkened not unto them; as the LORD had said. Exodus 7:10-13

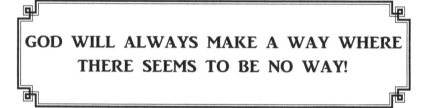

GOD WILL ALWAYS MAKE A WAY WHERE THERE SEEMS TO BE NO WAY!

The magician's rods also became serpents, and *pharmakia* was introduced. *Pharmakeia* is the Greek word translated pharmacy, which is "the making of medications." It also refers to the making of spell-giving potions or alchemical potions, which are believed to have transforming powers. These powers were thought to extend life, boost energy, or enhance the mind. *Pharmakeia* also refers to any substance used to poison someone, prevent or treat diseases, or to gain control of someone's behavior.

An interesting fact is that originally all medicines come from plants. God gave Adam dominion over the plant kingdom, but his disobedience reversed their healing properties and caused them to become killing properties. Don't get me wrong, I believe in medicines, but I believe more in the fact that if you will reverse the curse and get to the root of truth, then you can be healed. Medicines mask the symptoms and prolong the healing. I tell my clients to continue their medicines until the truth is unmasked. The medicine will run into the truth.

The modern transliteration of *pharmakeia* is *pharmacia*. This word appears several times in the New Testament (Galatians 5:20, Revelation 9:21, 18:23, 21:8 and 22:15). It is frequently referred to as *sorcery* or *witchcraft* and is listed among *"the works of the flesh."*

The Greek word *pharmakia* means *"drugs."* More then four hundred years ago, there were witches and sorcerers instead of pharmacists. Drugs were not used for healing, but were commonly used in pagan worship to cause hallucinations or to enable men to get in touch with evil spirits. Understand, I am not calling pharmacists witches and sorcerers; I am sharing the insights God gave me on *pharmakeia* and the dumb and deaf spirit. It wasn't until later that scientist studied different plants and chemicals and the effects they had on evil afflictions, and this brought about an understanding of what drugs can help with what diseases.

126

The truth is that soul holes are to blame for inviting afflictions into the body. Once we allow holes to form in our souls, afflictions can come in. We go to the physician, get a diagnosis, and then are prescribed a drug to solve the problem, but the problem is the holes in our soul.

The body manifests afflictions, and the soul manifests emotions. We wouldn't even have a need for medicine if our souls were not sick. If we get our soul holes healed, then our bodies will line up with the truth.

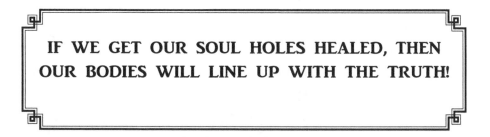

IF WE GET OUR SOUL HOLES HEALED, THEN OUR BODIES WILL LINE UP WITH THE TRUTH!

Med means Medicine, "Med-I-SIN." We need meds because of sin! "MED-I-SIN":

> *For the wages of sin is death, but the grace of God is eternal life in Christ Jesus our Lord.*   Romans 6:23

This might explain generational iniquities as well:

> *Keeping mercy for thousands, letting go of iniquity and rebellion and sin; and by no means will I absolve the guilty, visiting the iniquity of the fathers upon the sons and upon the sons' sons, unto the third and to the fourth generation.*   Exodus 34:7

Medical professionals have picked up on this wisdom concerning ancestors. One of the first things doctors ask you for is the medical history of your parents and grandparents. It's generational.

The problem with medicines is that they treat the symptoms but mask the problem. Don't misunderstand me. If I have a headache, I take Tylenol. If I have an infection, I use antibiotics. I thank God for medicines that help us when we are ill. However, I am simply sharing with you some insights concerning the original evil intentions that have affected mankind.

This gets tricky when it comes to medicine. I have heard people say, "God healed them," and they stop taking their medicine, but they're not healed. I have also heard people say, "If God wants to heal me, He can do it while I'm still on my medicine." Don't be foolish enough to say that God has healed you when you're just hoping He has. You will know when He heals you.

Your healing will come from a filling, not a feeling. Your healing is a fill, not a pill. We must *peel* the layers of pain back, face our soul hole foe, be filled and then flow. God revealed this insight to me so that I might receive understanding on how the evil tries to take us out.

In other words, chemotherapy has helped a lot of people live, but chemotherapy has killed more people than it has helped. We just need to have peace and understanding from God to be able to see the truth. Most people, once they are diagnosed with cancer, operate out of fear and fall prey to the dumb and deaf spirit by not knowing what to do. They can't hear God instruct them because they have fear of the diagnoses, and then, because they can't get a clear answer, they don't know what to do. Personally, I take medicine while seeking God for my healing.

God will reveal hidden mysteries in my life as I seek Him for the truth, and during this process, He shows me where my soul has holes. As I repent, He then fills my soul holes with His glory, causing my healing to come.

I won't lie to you: seeking your healing can be very frustrating. But, believe me, it is worth it when your healing comes.

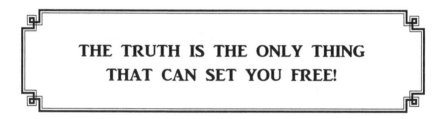

THE TRUTH IS THE ONLY THING THAT CAN SET YOU FREE!

A lady once told me that since she had been coming to my ministry, she had felt worse than ever. She had been on blood pressure meds for years. She played tennis several times a week and was in great shape, but her mom and dad both had high blood pressure, and her physician told her it was hereditary. We had been working on her soul holes for about six months, but she told me she was feeling worse. I advised her to go see her physician again.

The next time the woman came, she told me, "My body has regulated itself, and the blood pressure medication was now lowering my pressure too much, and that was why I felt so awful." Her medicine had run into her healing.

I don't look at the diagnosis; I seek a spiritual understanding of osmosis (os Moses). Lighten up! Don't judge me for the insight that God has revealed to me. There is always an underlying evil attempt to kill, steal, and destroy.

I believe that Moses had to deal with his fear, come out of denial, and allow God's glory to fill his soul holes. The goal is to get undammed and release the flow of God's glory. Remember, all of this occurred after Moses was introduced to that glory.

This is why it is so important to have a personal encounter with the King of Glory. When acknowledged, the glory will always bring revelation and insight to your confliction, addiction, and affliction. If you have an affliction and are seeking God for answers, may I lead you in a prayer?

Dear Heavenly Father,

I purpose and choose with my free will to repent for any and all fear, rejection, and abandonment that I have held in my heart as sin. I ask You to forgive me, and I forgive myself. I also forgive all others for the fear, rejection, and abandonment they have caused in my life. Lord, I ask that You show me insight and revelation concerning my affliction. Please reveal hidden mysteries to me about the origin of any evil that has attempted to affect my life. Father, show me any generational curses that may be upon my life, and show me how to be free from them now, in Jesus' name. Holy Spirit, please heal my broken heart and set me free. Lord, show me Your glory.

Amen!

Note: In order to hear God speak, you must listen carefully after every prayer for Him to give you clarity on your healing. God answers in many different ways. You may hear His voice, see a picture, smell an aroma, or have a memory. Keep your eyes closed, take a deep breath, and give God time to answer you in that still, small voice of His. You will be glad you did.

If you have not heard from God, then pray the prayer again and wait until He speaks. Don't try too hard. Your soul hole does not want you to hear God's voice, because when you do, you will be healed.

If you pray again and still do not hear from God, then you are dealing with an orphan soul hole, and we will address this in another chapter. Be encouraged as you are on the right track.

PHARMAKEIA

The dumb and deaf spirit must have something to do with *pharmakeia*. The medicine that we take keeps us from understanding the hidden mysteries that have been revealed. It is not the *med* as much as it is the *-icine* (I sin) part. We must get to the causes of our soul holes that could have come in by way of sin.

Fear, rejection, and abandonment are sins. We must have God's glory if these mysteries are going to be revealed to us. We must understand what we are dealing with in our soul and why. If we are going to be made whole, we can no longer afford to act as if we don't know what's going on.[7]

The reason I had a drug addiction wasn't because I was sick in my body; I was sick in my soul. No one had taught

---

7. Again, I discuss more about this in my pamphlet entitled **"The Dumb and Deaf Spirit."**

me about having soul holes. Therefore, I didn't understand that my soul needed healing. John said it best:

> *Beloved, I wish above all things that thou mayest prosper and be in health, even as thy soul prospereth.* 3 John 2

If our soul doesn't prosper, then our body won't prosper either.

When I was addicted to drugs, I was the last person to believe that I had a drug problem. I always fulfilled my daily responsibilities and achieved great accomplishments. I didn't know that I had a problem...until God revealed it to me. And He did not reveal it until I sought Him for help.

I was allowing *pharmakeia* to mask my soul holes. The task of a mask is to line up with your eye holes so that you can see out but no one can see in. Medicines mask the afflictions and thus keep you from looking into your soul, where God can reveal the truth and make you whole.

My soul holes demanded *pharmakeia* because I didn't understand the truth. As I identified the soul holes, I came out of denial, dealt with my undealt-with issues, humbled myself, and allowed the glory of God to reveal hidden mysteries. I got my soul holes filled, and the result was that I no longer needed the drugs to make me feel a certain way.

This was when I received understanding about my drug habit. The underlying emotional issue of addiction is the need to be loved. When I dedicated my life to the Lord, the church told me just to "give it all to God." When I would ask the leadership what this statement meant, all they could say was, "Give it all to God." I thought to myself, "I'm pretty sure that God doesn't want my dope!". God wants your hope, not your dope. Dope is the counterfeit of hope. How could I give God something that I didn't even know I had?

HOW DO YOU GIVE SOMETHING TO GOD WHEN YOU DON'T KNOW HOW?

Remember, *"lean not on thine own understanding."* As we identify the fear soul hole, we come out of agreement with the lie, we repent, and then we can be filled with the glory of God as the waters cover the sea.

The enemy is the opposite of what God has created, and he has caused us to see, hear, smell, taste, and feel the false instead of the true. When we turn it around, then (and only then) can we see, hear, smell, taste, and be FILLED by the truth. Fear must be identified as sin in order for us to be able to see the truth.

Someone might say, "Fear is not sin." Sin is anything you know you should not do, but you do it anyway:

> *Therefore to him that knoweth to do good, and do-eth it not, to him it is sin.*   James 4:17

The Word tells us many times, *"Fear not!"* So when we fear, guess what? We have just sinned. No one ever told me that fear was sin; they just said, "Give it to God." I needed to know how to give it to God. And, after I learned how to finally give my hope to God, then I had to learn how to leave it with Him.

If we're not careful, we give things to God and then take them back. Sin must be repented of. When we repent, we get set free from the fear. Maybe this is why so many Christians are full of fear! Now, let's move on to the next soul hole in the three-cord strand.

THE REJECTION CORD

Let us look at yet another devastating, dysfunctional soul hole—rejection. *Rejection* is "the dismissing or refusing of a proposal, idea, etc. ..., the spurning of a person's affections." *Rejection* can also be described as "one pushing another away." Rejection can come from family, friends, or even strangers. Rejection tells us that we are not accepted and that we will never belong. Shame and guilt drive rejection. The more rejection one operates under determines the amount of guilt and shame one experiences.

There are different degrees of rejection. These include: conversational rejection, congregational rejection, and sensational rejection. Regardless of the degree or the type, rejection hurts!

Rejection is the result of fear, and fear is the root of all rejection. Rejection and fear of rejection are two different issues. Rejection is a debilitating emotion in and of itself, but the fear of being rejected is the evidence that you have suffered rejection sometime in the past.

As we continue to learn about different negative emotions, remember: there is a difference between the emotion and the fear of the emotion. Feeling rejected is one of the most extreme of all emotions, and it is usually rooted in anger and bitterness. After anger and bitterness take root, jealousy and envy set in as well. Rejection tells us that, by human standards, we are undesirable.

Rejection is a sin. I know that rejection is a sin because the wages of sin is death, and rejection brings forth death. I have witnessed people who have rejected their healing miracle because of a lack of knowledge concerning rejection. Rejected people reject other people and then reject God's help.

Jesus was extremely rejected, which made it possible for us to have power and dominion over rejection:

> *He came unto his own, and his own received him not.*   John 1:11

Rejection causes us to place walls of self-protection around ourselves, to control the pain. When we have experienced rejection, we can neither give love completely nor receive love when it comes. Rejection thus produces double-mindedness.

There are two-types of rejection, either stemming from the root of rejection or from being rejected. They are self-rejection and rejection of others. We ultimately reject others because of our own self-rejection. We also reject ourselves and others when we have insecurities.

Once rejection has created a soul hole, many other holes can originate from this emptiness. Learn to reject rejection by replacing it with the truth of God:

Let your conversation be without covetousness; and be content with such things as ye have: for he hath said, I will never leave thee, nor forsake thee.

Hebrews 13:5

God has never rejected you. Therefore, you should never reject either yourself or others. Think of the lives of those people who have rejected you. It may not have been rejection; it could have been God's protection. Rejection is not worthy of accepting! If you have a hard time receiving, it is because you have a soul hole of rejection.

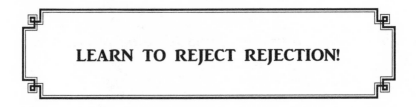

LEARN TO REJECT REJECTION!

Dear Heavenly Father,

I purpose and choose with my free will to repent for any and all ways that I have held rejection in my heart as sin. I ask You to forgive me, and I forgive myself for all the ways I have operated in rejection. I also forgive all others for the ways they have rejected me, and I release them all now, in Jesus' name.

Lord, I ask that You give me insight to reveal any hidden agendas of rejection, in Jesus' name. I ask that You forgive me for being insecure because of the sin of rejection. I come out of agreement with rejection now and ask You, Lord, to fill my soul hole of rejection.

Holy Spirit, please speak Your words of truth.

Amen!

This is also a prayer you can pray when fear and rejection try to come back and lie to you in an attempt to re-entangle you with their deceptions. God's truth will continue to change you from glory to glory.

Many times, you will need to continue to repent for whichever soul hole needs to be filled...until it gets filled. Soul holes can be dimensional. Therefore, keep seeking, repenting, and being filled, because one day soon you will overflow with your healing!

In other words, rejection is deeply rooted. Don't give up or give in. You've got this, as you move from glory to glory!

THE ABANDONMENT CORD

Fear sets in first and forms rejection, only to introduce you to abandonment. Abandonment is the BIG MAC DADDY! Physical and emotional *abandonment* are "the actions or facts of or being abandoned." *Emotional abandonment* is "an emotional state in which one feels left out, undesired, defected, discarded, and insecure."

Abandonment makes one feel left alone, withdrawn, and worthless. Abandonment's goal is to ostracize you from society. Abandonment is the highest form of rejection. Feelings of abandonment come after a person has experienced rejection, and a soul hole has been established. Abandoned orphans usually have the largest soul holes.

Always remember: there is the negative emotion of abandonment, and then there is the fear of actual abandonment. You couldn't have the fear of abandonment if you had not experienced real abandonment. The fear of abandonment causes more damage than the abandonment itself. Be aware of this difference when going through the prayers.

We were all adopted and grafted into the lineage of Jesus. Therefore, we must take notice of the enemy's attempt to influence us as orphans:

> *He came unto his own, and his own received him not. But as many as received him, to them gave he power to become the sons of God, even to them that believe on his name: which were born, not of blood, nor of the will of the flesh, nor of the will of man, but of God.* John 1:11-13

The truth is that we have all been accepted by the Father, but we must get our soul holes of abandonment filled and healed to walk in our eternal inheritance in the earthly realm.

We all know abandonment because we were once with God. We left His bosom to physically walk here on earth, as we work out our soul's salvation.

Abandonment has been perverted by evil (along with everything else) to make us think that we do not belong. You do belong, or you would not be here. Abandonment has a positive cause when we get set free from its negative effects. It causes us to run into the arms of God. While forsaking everything that has brought us security, we must trust Him with all our hearts, minds, and souls:[8]

> *And he answering said, Thou shalt love the Lord thy God with all thy heart, and with all thy soul, and with all thy strength, and with all thy mind; and thy neighbour as thyself.* Luke 10:27

If you have experienced extreme evil abandonment, then you will run with absolute abandonment to God and see things that you have only dreamed of seeing. Once the hidden mysteries of evil have been reversed, God can take you into the secret life of the Highest, and you will abide under the shelter of the Almighty (see Psalm 91).

OTHER ISSUES AT HAND

Now that we understand the original three-fold cord of disunity that causes most of our soul holes, let us continue to educate ourselves on the other issues at hand.

Have you ever met a person who must always be in control? A person who must be in control is being controlled by his or her soul holes. A hole in one's soul means that the hole is in control. The soul hole is damage that has been done but has not yet been dealt with.

For example, let's look at a soul hole of insecurity. *Insecurity* is "uncertainty or anxiety about oneself, or a lack of confidence." The soul hole of insecurity is the hole that

8. I write more on the good kind of abandonment in my book, **The High Place of God's Glory.**

security is lost in. If you have the soul hole of insecurity, security cannot operate.

In other words, the soul hole of insecurity is in control of your security. Self-control is a fruit of the Spirit:

> *But the fruit of the Spirit is love, joy, peace, forbearance, kindness, goodness, faithfulness, gentleness and self-control. Against such things there is no law.* Galatians 5:22-23, NIV

The opposite of self-control in the Spirit is a soul hole of control. A person will become controlling in the natural due to being out of control in the soul. Try not to think of others but apply this to your own life. I have a friend who is obsessively controlling. The truth is that he is being controlled by his many soul holes. He must be in control of every situation at all times. No one can tell him anything. His soul hole is out of control. Therefore, he tries to control everything and everybody around him.

As a result of this man's controlling issues, many people prefer not to be in his presence. Not only does he have control issues; he also has developed abandonment issues.

Keep in mind that the three soul holes that we have discussed are just a few of the many soul holes that desire to keep you from being made whole. When you start walking in your wholeness, you will be amazed at the life you will now live—a life of peace, health, wealth, and wisdom.

A PERSON WHO MUST BE IN CONTROL IS BEING CONTROLLED!

Dear Father God,

I purpose and choose with my free will to repent for all abandonment that I have operated in. I come out of agreement with abandonment and ask You to forgive me for the life of abandonment that I have lived. I forgive all others for abandoning me throughout my life, and I release them from any unforgiveness that I have formed in my heart as sin. I forgive myself for abandoning and neglecting myself. I break the generational curse of abandonment over myself and my family now, in Jesus' name. Lord, heal my soul hole of abandonment, and set me free.

In Jesus' name,
Amen!

Remember:

1. IDENTIFY SOUL HOLES
2. COME OUT OF DENIAL OF UNDEALT-WITH ISSUES AND EMOTIONS
3. HUMBLE YOURSELF, REPENT, AND ASK THE LORD TO FILL YOU WITH HIS GLORY

CHAPTER 5

DENYING AND DYING

And the serpent said unto the woman, Ye shall not surely die.   **Genesis 3:4**

Adam and Eve were never intended to taste death but to live forever. Unfortunately, they partook of the forbidden fruit and tasted death. I believe that the tree of life (in the center of the garden) must have been an olive tree, for Adam and Eve were supposed to <u>o-live</u> forever.

After the Fall of man, death would come as evidence of the detrimental decision of our ancestors. I believe that as they walked away from their O-live destiny, they fell short and ate a fig, which dis-<u>fig</u>ured them spiritually. After all, you are what you eat.

Instead of knowing all truth, they now had to figure things out for themselves. They hid behind fig leaves, and because of their sin, would now have to <u>fig</u>ure out who they had become. That one taste cost them their estate. Now, they would have to become the land that was cursed with formlessness and voids, an earth that would have to be filled with the glory of God as the waters cover the sea (see Habakkuk 2:14).

God created a fallen place to house a fallen race that would now have to face its sin...if they ever wanted to go back in. EVIL would now be the opposite of LIVE, and our lives would reflect the effect of sin.

Sin spelled backwards is *nis* which means *is not*. Nis is also the largest city in southern Serbia and the third largest city in Serbia. Nis is the administrative center of Nisava District. It is one of the oldest cities in the Balkans and in Europe, and from ancient times it has been considered to be a "gateway between the East and the West." Interesting, isn't it? It was also the birthplace of Constantine the Great, the first Christian Emperor.

In other words, our sins have kept us in a wilderness of wondering who we are, kept us from our original identity in God. Sin has made us the opposite of who God called us to be. Therefore, we must turn westward and go back into the place that our ancestors came out of, so that the curse can be reversed. Our skin came because of sin, and the veil would cover us...until we could enter back in.

Soul holes make us uncomfortable in our skin...until we unveil the sin. The hidden mystery is revealed, as we are unveiled, to the truth that will set us free from the forbidden fruit.

The word *evil* is also found in *veil*. The words, *iDENtity* and *eDEN* contain the word **DEN.** The definition of *den* is "a wild animal's habitation, a small, comfortable room in a house where a person can pursue an activity in private, and a small structure built by children as a place to play, hide, or provide shelter." Think of your life as a game of Hide and Go Seek. We are the hidden mystery, as we seek, we find the truth and are being set free to enter back in. As evidence of their fall, Adam and Eve came away from God and had to seek shelter in the wilderness. They would now have to seek God to find shelter in His presence.

To be healed, we must go the opposite way of sin. *Sin* spelled backward is *Nis* (the gateway between the East and West), which is where we must go to be restored back to our original identity. This gateway is the place of turning from sin and going back into the place which was first exited by Adam and Eve.

If sin made our ancestors go east, then we must go the opposite way, which would be west. If things aren't working for you, then it's time to turn and try a different way. You either take your way or Yahweh's! To find the peace of God, we must do this, even though it is in opposition to traditionalism and religion. Go west, young man! We must come out of **DEN**ial and become who God originally created us to be.

There are only two places where we can dwell: the desert of false identity or the Promised Land of true intimacy. Where are you dwelling?

GO WEST, YOUNG MAN

The dictionary defines *denial* as "the state of one that refuses the truth or existence of, refusing to give or grant something requested or desired to someone, to declare untrue, to refuse to admit or acknowledge, to give a negative answer, to restrain from." Does any of this sound familiar

145

to you? If you are reading this book, God is trying to set you free. Denial is a deadly emotion that automatically denies you access to eternal provisions. Many Christians live in denial. Believing truth separates a believer from a non-believer.

The truth, however, will not automatically set one free. It is believing the truth that sets one free, and this is why we are called believers. We must oppose man's way of figuring things out because figuring is a form of doubt. The truth does not have to be figured out, only believed. When we believe the truth, it sets us free.

The only advantage we can have over sin is to believe what the truth says so that we can be set free. We should see a major difference in our lives and the lives of unbelievers. Unfortunately, we don't see a lot of difference in our lives and others. The divorce rate among believers is the same as the divorce rate among unbelievers. Death by cancer is the same among believers as among unbelievers.

There must be a difference between believers and unbelievers, and the difference will come from getting soul holes filled. When we believe the truth of God, then we can become the truth of God. As a result, we will not only read the Word but become the Word. We either believe or we don't believe.

On their death beds, I see many people confessing that God is healing them, and then they die. If God is healing them, why do they die? We have learned to live with lies, and in God's defense, we justify our situations. I hear people asking, "Why doesn't God heal us?" God doesn't need us to defend Him. God needs someone to stand for the truth and get to the root of the afflictions that continue to steal, kill, and destroy. He needs us to deal with our soul holes and believe the truth and not lies.

God's intention is not to just heal us; His intention is that we never become sick. Lies are real, but we need to REALIZE (real lies) that they are not the truth. We make up things when we really don't know the truth. We say things such as, "God knows the whole picture." Yes, God does know the WHOLE picture, and He would like for us to know the WHOLE picture as well.

Unfortunately, we know more about holes than wholeness. God desires that our souls be made whole. He desires that we know soul wholeness.

If you are to dwell in the Promised Land of true identity, then you cannot afford to try to figure it all out. Our true identity is true intimacy, and anything else leaves one afflicted. The truth does not have to be figured out; figuring is something we do because of our doubts. The truth must simply be believed.

Believe (unveil the lie to be). We were taught the A B C's early in life. I am discovering the opposite C B A. C (see), B (be), the A (apple). We are the apple of God's eye:

> *Keep me as the apple of the eye, hide me under the shadow of thy wings.*   Psalm 17:8

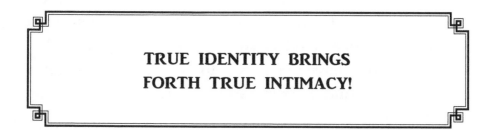

TRUE IDENTITY BRINGS FORTH TRUE INTIMACY!

Emptiness is the evidence of deception. We have been empty for so long that we defend our emptiness by thinking that it's a part of our individuality. You were not created to be empty! God is not empty, so why should we be empty? We do need to be emptied of every negative emotion that has tried to steal our identity. We end up empty because soul holes have disabled us from containing the presence of God.

We defend our emptiness because our soul holes have become our friends. Fear tells you, "Protect yourself!" Rejection tells you, "Don't be open to others, or they will hurt you!" And abandonment tells you, "No one understands you, so you will always be alone." These are just a few of the lies our soul holes tell us, to keep us from being filled with the truth.

Our soul holes know when we repent and come out of agreement with them. The only chance they have is in Hell. We listen to our soul hole lies, and then we justify the deception, which keeps us incarcerated to our own deceptive conditions. This is where denial comes in.

Have you ever been asked, "Are you telling the whole truth?" The truth is whole, but lies create holes. We deny the truth that will set us free because we are afraid that if we give up what we have, we will be left as orphans with nothing.

An orphan owns nothing and has no hope of things becoming any different from the way they have always been. Does that sound familiar? You can have an orphan heart without being orphaned by your parents. Parents came because sin had to have two halves to make a whole. Parents just rent their children from God (pair-rent). God owns all our children.

We must be able to discern the truth from a lie. This has been a problem from the time of Grandfather Adam and Grandmother Eve. This is our "iniquit-inheritance" from our ancestors because they would not face the truth. Iniquities are no more than in-i-quit-ties (IN I QUIT TIES)! I am ready to quit what I am tied to and receive both the righteous inheritance of the Lord and everything else that God has promised me here on this earth:

> *Giving thanks unto the Father, which hath made us meet to be partakers of the inheritance of the saints in light.* Colossians 1:12

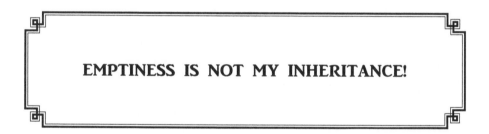

EMPTINESS IS NOT MY INHERITANCE!

THE WHOLE TRUTH

Wholeness comes when we know the truth, believe the truth, and get set free by the truth. The truth itself cannot set us free unless we believe it for ourselves. To walk in the truth, we must separate ourselves from the lies that tie us to the soul holes. Come out of the hole to be made whole. Sin is the lie, and if we lie (sin), we cannot be set free.

The reason we are slow to disbelieve the lie is because it has lied to us as if it were our friend. If I must believe a lie in order to have a friend, I would rather be friendless. Jesus is a Friend to the friendless.

Unfortunately, we have justified deadly situations with half-truths. We have believed the lie because we don't really know the whole truth. I have heard people say, "If it be God's will to heal me, I will be healed." We don't know the whole truth, or we could believe it and be healed. The whole truth is, that it is not God's will to heal you. The whole truth will make you whole. God's will is that you never become sick.

We make excuses for God because we don't want Him to look like He only heals certain people. When we are in denial and don't know the truth, we try to defend God when bad things happen to good people. We must go back to the original intention of God and seek the truth of His purpose. How did Adam and Eve first fall short? Was it because of food that God said not to eat? We have been out of order with our eating ever since.

When we are out of order, we form disorders. Food disorders are soul holes that desire to be filled. If you are at the point that you cannot lose weight, it may be because your soul hole needs to be healed. Most people live to eat, but we are supposed to eat to live. You are what you eat. People are dying prematurely because of what they choose to eat, and then God gets blamed for the lie that caused them to die.

OVEREATING IS DUE TO THE EMPTINESS OF OUR SOULS!

We, as humans, usually justify our behaviors and commonly speak in a third person manner, thus covering up our wrongs. The reason we speak in third person is we know better, but we choose to deny the truth. We know what we should be doing or thinking, but we get around the truth by verbally justifying not doing what we know we should be doing. If we verbalize it, we somehow think we can excuse ourselves from being accountable.

If we excuse and justify our soul holes, we can never become holy. Example: I know that I should not eat an extra-fudge chocolate sundae, but eat it anyway. Blatant rebellion demands a high price when it comes time to reap the consequences. Consciously, we excuse our wrongs to give ourselves permission to partake of things we know are not healthy.

Being healthy is a benefit of becoming whole. This humanistic behavior has been taught throughout our previous generations as a way of getting around the truth. If not attended to before it is passed on to the future generations, they will grow calloused because they will not be operating in the truth that God has made available for them to be set free. Then we wonder why the next generation has a hard time hearing the voice of God.

151

Every truth of God that we ignore and every time that we operate in our own desires, we make the next generation prone to denying the same truths. As this disobedience grows with each generation, the disobedience and cravings increase.

In other words, it might not be an extra-fudge chocolate sundae, but a line of cocaine that satisfies your child's cravings. The bottom line is that we must deal with our soul holes and be set free from the things that try to steal, kill, and destroy us.

We are the generation that can reverse the curse, so that we and our children can live free of evil. We must stop identifying with the things we should not be doing by justifying them and by refusing to change. The greatest asset we have to offer eternity is our ability to change while here on earth.

Denial is deadly. We must seek the truth, believe it, and allow it to set us free.

A father who falls prey to pornography may be his son's future justification for having extra-marital affairs. The things that we sweep under the rug will be the very things that our children trip over. Soul holes are transferable to our children. What we won't deal with will deal with our children and grandchildren.

Dear Heavenly Father,

I purpose and choose with my free will to repent for not dealing with my "stuff." Lord, I ask that You forgive me for all the times that I have done what I desired to do, even though Your truth was evident to me. Please forgive me for justifying my wrongs by telling myself that I can go ahead and do what I want to without having any accountability or consequences.

Lord, any way that I look at this, it's rebellion! Rebellion is as the sin of witchcraft, and witchcraft is the origin of medicine. I see the truth; however, I have blamed You for not blessing me in certain areas of my life, when it was my disobedience that brought forth my demise. I forgive myself for dodging the truth, so that my selfishness could prosper. Give me the strength to face myself head on, so that I may be set free by Your truth, in Jesus' name. I forgive all others for teaching me how to evade the truth when I did not want to hear it.

Holy Spirit, please speak Your words of truth, and set me free from me.   Amen!

THE PROOF IS IN THE TRUTH

When the truth is clear in my life, then I will be better able to help others see the truth in their lives. I can't give someone a clean cup of water if I'm dipping out of a muddy well. If we truly love, then that love is truth, and it will help the captives get set free. The only qualification we must have to help others be set free is that we must first be set free ourselves. I did not say "perfect"; I said "free."

This is not a religious act; this is a revelatory act. A religious act is saying you are going to do better; a revelatory act is doing better.

No one will listen to you if they do not see the evidence of your freedom. You must have the revelation and insight from God to be set free before you can help others get set free.

If you need a haircut, you go to a hair salon. If you need an oil change, you go to a garage. If you need to be set free, you go to someone who is free. Free people tell you the truth because it was the truth that set them free.

One of the greatest rules in my life is this:

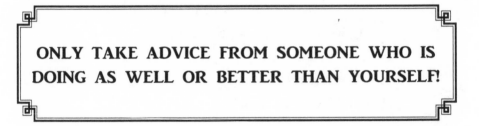

ONLY TAKE ADVICE FROM SOMEONE WHO IS DOING AS WELL OR BETTER THAN YOURSELF!

If those who believe are operating in the truth, then peace and prosperity should follow. The proof is in the pudding! The proof is in the truth. You don't have to defend truth; it speaks for itself.

You cannot fake being healed; you either are or you are not. You cannot fake being happy, prosperous, or stable. If you do not have peace and prosperity, then you must find the soul holes that are depriving you of these promises.

The only way to get to your promises fulfilled and live an abundant life is to come out of denial and allow the truth to set you free.

Any fake area in our lives is evidence of a soul hole. Life in general tells us, when we fall, "Get back up! You're not hurt!" Then we live the rest of lives acting like we're not hurt! But if something hurts, let it hurt. Then, find what you are looking for and be set free. Don't deny the hurt and die prematurely because the hurt has grown roots of bitterness that eventually attract disease. Come out of agreement with, stop denying that it did hurt, repent of the pain, and be healed.

Dear Heavenly Father,

I purpose and choose with my free will to repent for all ways that I have denied my pain. I acknowledge that (call the person's name, if necessary) hurt me, and I never allowed myself time to deal with the pain. I come out of agreement with the lie that I am all right when I'm not, and I give myself permission to explore the hurt.

Lord, give me the strength not to get stuck in self-pity, as I plunder through the ruins of my emotions while seeking to find the truth that will set me free. I forgive myself and all others for the pain I have caused and the pain that others have caused me, in Jesus' name.

Lord, give me insight that will help me to understand my process of healing. Holy Spirit, please speak Your words of truth.

Amen!

The only two letters that are different in *denying* and *dying* are **"en."** The prefix *en* is used to change adjectives and nouns into verbs. *En* (or in) can also be used as a prefix in a number of verbs like **in**corporate, **in**clude, **in**vite, **in**volve, etc. *En* means "**in**."

En also means to come into and is used as a suffix to form transitive and intransitive verbs from adjectives (hard**en**, sweet**en**), or from nouns (deep**en**, strength**en**). In other words, this *en* has the ability to change things for your soul. Take the *en* out of denial, and then you can **dial** up God!

God is the only one you can call on to heal your soul holes. We need to allow the truth to come **in**to our souls and fill the holes that have been formed by the pains and traumas in life. I love the story that begins in 2 Kings 7:3:

> *And there were four leprous men at the entering in of the gate: and they said one to another, Why sit we here until we die?*

We must be as desperate as the lepers were in this passage of scripture. Their disease was contagious and could infect others. Therefore, they were placed outside of the camp. Sometimes our soul holes place us on the outside of the camp in the form of rejection and abandonment. We must be desperate enough to go **in**to our healing.

It will take courage to go into the places of pain in your soul that you have learned to accept. Think about the fact that your soul holes are contagious and are affecting others, just as your parents' soul holes affected you. Therefore, you must get healed, or your soul holes will affect your children and others.

Fear, rejection, and abandonment have put us on the out-side of our own souls. Get back on the inside of your soul, and take control of every soul hole, thus assuring that the pain stops here.

Why must you sit here until you die? Rise up! Take the camp of your healing that has been confiscated by your soul holes, and take back what the lies have stolen! For the truth to set you free, you must let truth come **in**to your soul, so that it can separate you from the issues that keep you from being made whole.

Truth cannot set you free unless you allow it to come **in**to your soul. If your soul holes have closed you up emotionally, then you must open up in order to be healed.

Jesus helped a mute man with his soul holes in Mark 7:34-35:

> *And looking up to heaven, he sighed, and saith unto him, Ephphatha, that is, Be opened. And straight-way his ears were opened, and the string of his tongue was loosed, and he spake plain.*

In other words, the man was healed of the dumb and deaf spirit that had closed his soul from hearing and understand-ing God. We must now be opened because our soul holes have kept us closed for far too long. Because we are so full of fear, we have operated in our brokenness and have defended our soul holes. Why must we sit here until we die?

Denial is dangerous. Denial is the greatest enemy to the truth because denial will not give the truth a chance to set the captives free. Denial is the gateway to death. You will eventually die from what you deny.

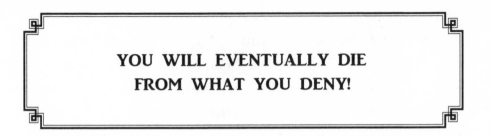

YOU WILL EVENTUALLY DIE FROM WHAT YOU DENY!

Denial is just a fancy word for lie. The goal is to come out of denial and then die to whatever caused us to deny. We must come out of denial to accept the truth. To set you free, the truth needs a place to land within your soul. If we live in denial, chances are we will die in denial. When we come out of denial and face the soul hole, we can then be made whole.

Denial will grant deception a right to occupy your soul. Denial is usually the doorway through which the lie enters. Denial gives you a place to hide your sin. We fear truth because our established soul hole indentions influence deceptions that are deeper than our current reality.

The soul hole of fear tells you one thing, while the spirit inside of you is trying to bring you into a place of release. Your spirit is a form of witness for your soul.

Your spirit cannot operate in denial because it is the part of you that has been with God. An atheist can deny God with His soul, but it is impossible for him to deny Christ Jesus with his spirit. Your spirit is the truth of your inner man. However, if you keep denying God, your spirit will, over time, conform to your soul.

The only way you can break your spirit is by denying God with your soul, and this will cause your broken spirit to grieve. David experienced this broken spirit:

> *The sacrifices of God are a broken spirit: a broken and a contrite heart, O God, thou wilt not despise.*
> Psalm 51:17

If we continue to put off dealing with our soul holes, there is a good chance that our spirit will be broken. Believe me when I say that a soul hole is easier to deal with than a broken spirit.

When Christians disobey God, they disobey Him out of their soul, not their spirit. Remember, it is important to get our soul holes filled, because the more holes it has, the weaker it becomes, thus making it more prone to deception, that causes death. We call ourselves believers, and then we deny both God and His truth by allowing our soul holes to remain. God is love, and love is truth. Soul holes are the evidence of believers denying the truth. If we love God, then we must learn to love truth:

> *If a man say, I love God, and hateth his brother, he is a liar: for he that loveth not his brother whom he hath seen, how can he love God whom he hath not seen?*
> 1 John 4:20

This shows the untruth of the matter. We should believe, instead of forming soul holes out of our doubts, disobedience, and denial.

SOUL HOLES ARE THE EVIDENCE
OF A DIS-EASED SOUL!

I have ministered to many people in abusive relationships. The question I ask all of them is, "Why do you stay?" It baffles my mind as to why anyone would stay in an abusive relationship. If you knew that a car was going to run over you, would you get out in the road? Soul holes of fear, rejection, and abandonment tell these people that "something is better than nothing." In other words, being in an abusive relationship is better than not having anyone at all. This is a lie!

Our soul holes tell us lies to keep us in situations that control and manipulate our minds. These are real lies, but we need to realize that they are only lies. This is also true of toxic friends. We tolerate toxic people because we fear being alone.

I have an old friend who once told me that she liked me better before I got my soul holes healed. I answered her, "What you liked was treating me unkindly and getting away with it." I had tolerated the way she treated me because I was broken. When you get healed, you will no longer tolerate people treating you unkindly.

My grandmother was in a verbally abusive relationship for years before I finally asked her, "Why do you tolerate him treating you like he does?"

Like many, she said, "It was better than being alone."

The more broken you are, the more abuse you will tolerate from others. The more healed you become, the more you will be able to love yourself and release others.

Many times we blame the devil for things that our soul holes tell us. The liar may not be the enemy. Instead, the lie is in-a-me, and that keeps me from being a-live. My true enemy is me. It is what is in me. I am my own worst enemy.

Liar spelled backward is *RAIL*. The liar will de-rail you from the truth.

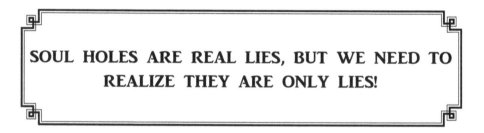

SOUL HOLES ARE REAL LIES, BUT WE NEED TO REALIZE THEY ARE ONLY LIES!

God asked Adam, "Where are you, and who told you that you were naked?"

Adam avoided answering with the truth, because the lie had entered him and had caused him to hide. The seeds of the deceit had taken root inside of Adam and Eve, and they would now have to sprout and grow. Whatever you deny will be the thing that you will hide behind and then reproduce.

Soul holes cannot tell the truth because they are lies that hide deep inside our souls. Adam blamed Eve for giving him the fruit. Then he blamed God for giving him the woman. In other words, they once were whole, but then they became two halves. They now began to blame each other. Instead of being filled, they began to feel empty.

We hear husbands and wives referring to each other as their "better half." You never hear them call each other their "worst half." If you walk in denial, you will always blame God or others for your guilt and shame.

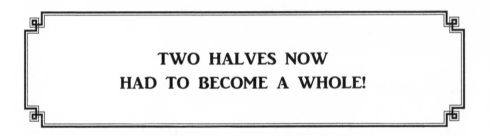

**TWO HALVES NOW
HAD TO BECOME A WHOLE!**

Soul holes have been a part of our souls for such a long time that we often have a hard time discerning the truth. Discernment is knowing the difference between good and evil. Mature discernment is choosing good. We have been given a free will that allows us to achieve anything we put our minds to:

> *And the LORD said, Behold, the people is one, and they have all one language; and this they begin to do: and now nothing will be restrained from them, which they have imagined to do.*   Genesis 11:6

The will that God placed within our soul is joined in unity with our spirit and body and is the part of us that can do all things. It takes the truth to line up all three aspects to produce peaceful people who are equipped to fulfill what God has called them to do.

I have seen people will themselves to live in seemingly-impossible situations. I have also seen people will themselves to die. If we can see it in our minds, we can achieve it with our hearts. Why don't we deal with the deepest, darkest secrets of our soul and be made whole?

> *I can do all things through Christ which strength-*
> *eneth me.*   Philippians 4:13

We like to quote the scripture, *"I can do all things,"* but if we can, then why don't we? It is a matter of identifying our soul holes, coming out of denial of undealt-with issues and emotions, humbling ourselves, and repenting, so the glory of God can heal us.

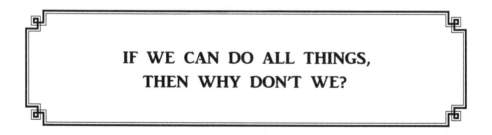

**IF WE CAN DO ALL THINGS,
THEN WHY DON'T WE?**

It's time to rise out of the ashes of our ruins and walk in the beauty and splendor of God Almighty. Coming out of denial will be like the Israelites coming out of Egypt. God will make sure that we have all that we need to be free. He gave the Israelites jewels and supernatural clothing and shoes because He loved them so much:

> *And I have led you forty years in the wilderness: your clothes are not waxen old upon you, and thy shoe is not waxen old upon thy foot.*
>
> Deuteronomy 29:5

> *But every woman shall borrow of her neighbour, and of her that sojourneth in her house, jewels of silver, and jewels of gold, and raiment: and ye shall put them upon your sons, and upon your daughters; and ye shall spoil the Egyptians.* Exodus 3:22

Through Jesus Christ, we have everything we need to overcome any and all soul holes. The challenge is: can we identify the soul holes and come out of denial, in order to be able to overcome the death that they bring to our minds, bodies, and souls? Are you ready to be made whole?

Dear Heavenly Father,

I purpose and choose with my free will to repent for all lies that I have held in my heart as sin. Lord, forgive me as I forgive myself for lying to You, myself, and others. I was afraid of the truth because I believed the lies. Help me to discern the truth from the lies. I repent of any fear I have had concerning evicting all lies from my soul. Lord, help me come out of denial and be able to deal with all of my undealt-with issues. I desire to align my spirit, body, and soul with Your truths. I forgive all others for teaching me how to lie to myself. I release everyone who has lied to me, and I break any soul ties that I have or have had with anyone, in Jesus' name.

Holy Spirit please speak Your words of truth.

Amen!

Remember, to be free:

1. IDENTIFY YOUR SOUL HOLES
2. COME OUT OF THE DENIAL OF UNDEALT-WITH ISSUES AND EMOTIONS
3. HUMBLE YOURSELF, REPENT, AND ASK THE LORD TO FILL YOU WITH HIS GLORY

CHAPTER 6

NAME IT, BUT DON'T BLAME IT

For all have sinned and come short of the glory of
God.   Romans 3:23

Why do we automatically blame other people when we fall short of God's glory? I believe it is generational. Papa Adam blamed Nanny Eve for giving him the fruit, and the blame game was on. If that were not enough, as we have seen, Adam turned around and blamed God for giving him the woman:

> *And the man said, The woman whom thou gavest*
> *to be with me, she gave me of the tree, and I did eat.*
>   Genesis 3:12

When we fall short and walk in false identity, we tend to blame others, to get the monkey off of our own back. Chances are the monkey is on your back because you decided to carry him. If we blame other people, we are not making ourselves available to be set free to walk in our true identity. Stop trying to get the monkey off your back, and deal with the monkey face to face. The mon-key may be the key to the mon (man).

A MAN WHO BLAMES ANOTHER WILL NEVER DISCOVER OR RECOVER!

We automatically blame others because we don't understand why we fall short. We hide behind our pride in hopes of others not finding out the truth. As a child, do you remember arguing with others and saying, "I know what you are, but what am I?" Those were your soul holes reflecting whatever was said to you by saying it back to others.

Hurtful words that are spoken toward us are usually received by our soul holes. Then, we send those hurtful words back out because of the pain they caused us when they were received.

Soul holes love to mirror each other. For example, when someone rejects you, your soul hole rejects them. When you get your soul hole healed, hurtful words have nowhere to land.

I have often heard people say, "If I could change myself, I would." The truth is that we are the only ones who can change ourselves. The fact of the matter is that our soul hole makes us think we can't change ourselves. This is a lie from

Hell. God has granted us all authority here on earth as it is in Heaven, and we are more than able to change.

If we don't change in a voluntary state of mind, the other option will kick in. Our body will change involuntary. In other words, change while you still can because if you don't your soul holes will cause afflictions in your body that will bring a forced change. This information will give you options for healing. You are not alone.

Soul holes could be the reason our bodies form holes that hide from our healing. We must seek the truth and identify our soul holes, and stop blaming others for our destructive decisions and behavior. Every hole in your soul tries to blame other people or things so that they can remain. Be careful of the "they-sayers." "They-sayers" are usually people of unknown origin. In fact, "they-sayers" are usually the voices of other people's soul holes!

Often, people come and tell me negative things that others have said about me, but when I ask them who said these hurtful things, they say, "They said." Who are they? They never have a name because "they" have no identity (no truth). So, why do we give "them" so much power?

We need to name the evil and stop blaming others for the pain that we experience. Name it, but don't blame it. Each soul hole has a name. We must identify the soul hole, stop blaming other people, take accountability, and identify the soul hole that is causing the pain.

The real reason we blame others for our pain is because we don't want to take accountability for it. I would like to help you learn how to take accountability for your pain. If it is your pain, it belongs to you, and no one else can get rid of it for you. So, stop blaming others for causing your pain and stop expecting others to heal your pain. God is the only One that can heal you.

If a person hurts me, it is my fault. I know this is contrary to what we usually think, but the soul hole was there before the other person was. No one can hurt me if I don't have a soul hole, and it is my responsibility to deal with my soul holes. It is easy to blame others when, in reality, is your own fault. Deal with your soul hole, and stop blaming others. Identify the soul hole, come out of denial, humble yourself, repent, and be set free.

A few examples of soul holes are lack of identity, addiction, fear in general, fear of man, fear of rejection, anxiety, and hope deferred. When we can identify with the soul holes and blame the lie, then we can be set free to be all that God has created us to be. We blame others because we don't know how to take responsibility for our own evil actions. God's children are destroyed for lack of knowledge. What is in me is the author of my pain. Therefore, gain knowledge of the evil that is at work, repent, and allow the glory of God to heal your soul. This will probably take up a whole chapter in itself, but will, by far, be the most important chapter in the whole book.

Let us look at the different soul holes, understand their actions, and stop the vicious cycle of blame. Name it, don't blame it. I will share twelve common afflictions (things that are dis-ease to the soul). These examples are just a taste of the truth that will set us free once we receive this knowledge.

My next up-coming book will list hundreds of soul holes, how to identify them, repent, and be healed. Remember, if it is not good and perfect, it is not from God:

> *Every good gift and every perfect gift is from above, and cometh down from the Father of lights, with whom is no variableness, neither shadow of turning.* James 1:17

First, we will define the affliction, and then we will identify the soul hole so that we will know what to repent of. After we identify the soul hole, we will pray a prayer of repentance and then listen for God to give us more insight into how to be set free.

Each time, I will be using a model prayer that I adapted from Dr. Art Mathias. This prayer states that you are purposely choosing, with your own free will, to identify the soul holes, defining the afflictions attached to them (so you can come out of agreement with them), repenting of sins associated with them, and calling forth God's insight to bring you understanding concerning the healing of your soul.

Immediately after I finish writing this book, I will start writing the sequel to it entitled *Whole Soul*. The second book will address knowledge and information about hundreds of soul holes.

My friend, you are about to embark upon your journey of wholeness, so that you can receive the healing that your heart has desired. You are the well of God's glory unveiled, and finally, you are about to be made whole.

AFFLICTION—ACNE

DEFINITION—The occurrence of inflamed or infected sebaceous glands in the skin; a condition characterized by red pimples on the face, which is prevalent chiefly among teenagers.

SOUL HOLES THAT MAY CAUSE ACNE: anxiety, fear, rejection of peers, insecurity, lack of identity, addiction, hope deferred, fear of man, depression.

A MODEL PRAYER FOR ACNE:

> Dear Heavenly Father,
>
> I purpose and choose with my free will to repent of anxiety, fear, rejection of peers, insecurity, lack of identity, addiction, hope deferred, fear of man, and depression. I ask You to forgive me, and I forgive myself and come out of agreement with all these sins, in Jesus' name.
> I also forgive everyone who has ever hurt me in these negative emotions, and I command acne to go, in Jesus' name.
> Holy Spirit, please heal my brokenness, and speak Your words of truth, and set me free.

Note: You must be willing to remain silent after each prayer in order to hear the Holy Spirit speak His words of truth.

His voice may be an image, a thought, a memory, or even an aroma. Never underestimate how God can communicate with those who have an ear to hear.

Don't be too religious in these prayers because I may not say amen at the end. Sometimes, I will not say amen because we need the prayer to extend into our full understanding. I have found that if we say amen at the end, people often won't remain open to hear from God. That amen closes the issue for them.

Amen means agreement with truth, or "truly." Unfortunately, amen at the end of a prayer religiously can stop you from receiving the understanding that God has to offer. Amen is not the end; amen is the beginning of truth. You need to hear from God more than you need to hear from a-man.

AFFLICTION—<u>ARTHRITIS</u>

DEFINITION—The painful inflammation and stiffness of the joints.

SOUL HOLES THAT MAY CAUSE ARTHRITIS: fear, anxiety, anger, stress, self-bitterness, self-hatred, guilt, and extreme bitterness.

A MODEL PRAYER FOR ARTHRITIS:

Dear Heavenly Father,

I purpose and choose with my free will to repent of fear, anxiety, anger, stress, self-bitterness, self-hatred, guilt, and extreme bitterness. I ask You to forgive me, and I forgive myself and come out of agreement with all of these negative emotions, in Jesus' name. I also forgive all others for any way they have hurt me. I come out of agreement with arthritis now, in Jesus' name. I cancel this debt of arthritis, in Jesus' name.

Holy Spirit, please speak Your words of truth, and set me free from me.

AFFLICTION—<u>ASTHMA</u>

DEFINITION—A respiratory condition marked by spasms in the bronchi of the lungs, causing difficulty in breathing. It usually results from an allergic reaction or other forms of hypersensitivity.

SOUL HOLES THAT MAY CAUSE ASTHMA: fear, fear of rejection, rejection, fear of abandonment, and worry

A MODEL PRAYER FOR ASTHMA:

Dear Heavenly Father,

I purpose and choose with my free will to repent of fear, fear of rejection, rejection, fear of abandonment, and worry. I ask You to forgive me, and I forgive myself and come out of agreement with all these negative emotions, in Jesus' name. I also forgive all others for the way they have hurt me, and I come out of agreement with asthma now, in Jesus' mighty name.

Holy Spirit, please speak Your words of truth, and set me free.

AFFLICTION—BREAST CANCER

DEFINITION—Breast cancer is a disease in which cells in the breast grow out of control. There are different kinds of breast cancer. Most breast cancers begin in the ducts or lobules. Breast cancer can spread outside of the breast through blood vessels and lymph vessels.

SOUL HOLES THAT MAY CAUSE BREAST CANCER: fear, fear of cancer, stress, self-conflict, unresolved issues, bitterness toward others, and false burden bearing (carrying the heaviness of others on your chest).

A MODEL PRAYER FOR BREAST CANCER:

Dear Heavenly Father,

I purpose and choose with my free will to repent for all ways I have held fear, all fear of cancer, stress, self-conflict, unresolved issues with other females, false burden bearing, and bitterness in my heart as sin. Lord, I ask that You forgive me, and I forgive myself and all others for hurting me. Lord, please bring to my remembrance

175

the origin of this evil disease that has afflicted my body, that I may be able to repent and enter into my healing. Teach me how to humble myself as I allow Your truth to penetrate my soul and make me whole. I cancel this debt of breast cancer, in Jesus' name.

I ask You, Holy Spirit, to please heal my broken heart and speak Your words of truth, in Jesus' name.

AFFLICTION—CHRONIC BACK PAIN

DEFINITION—Chronic back pain is defined as pain that persists for twelve weeks or longer, even after an initial injury or underlying cause of acute low back pain has been treated. About twenty percent of people affected by acute low back pain develop chronic low back pain with persistent symptoms in one year.

SOUL HOLES THAT MAY CAUSE CHRONIC BACK PAIN: anxiety, anger, "drivenness," worry, bitterness, fear, hope deferred, and false burden bearing

A MODEL PRAYER FOR CHRONIC BACK PAIN:

Dear Heavenly Father,

I purpose and choose with my free will to repent for all fear, anxiety, anger, "drivenness," worry, bitterness, and hope deferred that I have held in my soul. Lord, I ask that You forgive me for false burden bearing and carrying the burdens of others. Lord, my job is not to carry the burdens of others, and I am sorry for the way I have tried to play God.

I also forgive others for placing false expectations on my life that have made me feel like I was responsible for their lives. Please forgive me, and I forgive myself for operating out of my brokenness. I understand now that this is the reason my back feels broken. I cancel this debt of chronic back pain, in Jesus' name, and I ask You, Holy Spirit, to speak Your words of truth.

AFFLICTION—CHRONIC EAR INFECTION

DEFINITION—Chronic ear infection is fluid, swelling, or an infection behind the eardrum that does not go away or keeps coming back. It can cause long-term or permanent damage to the ear. It most often involves a hole in the eardrum that does not heal.

SOUL HOLES THAT MAY CAUSE CHRONIC EAR INFECTION: rejection from the father, fear, inherited fear of abandonment, insecurities, accusation, and a spirit of infirmity

A MODEL PRAYER FOR CHRONIC EAR INFECTION:

Dear Heavenly Father,

I purpose and choose with my free will to repent for

rejection from my earthly father, fear, inherited fear of abandonment, insecurities, accusation, and the spirit of infirmity. Lord, I ask that You forgive me, and I forgive myself. I also forgive all others for any way they have caused me pain, in Jesus' name.

Father, I ask that You show me Your truth, and set me free from any issues that concern my fears. Holy Spirit, please speak Your words of truth to me and set me free.

AFFLICTION—CHRONIC FATIGUE SYNDROME

DEFINITION—The main symptom is fatigue lasting over six months. The fatigue often worsens with activity and doesn't improve with rest. This condition is also known as Systemic Exertion Intolerance Disease (SEID) or Myalgic Encephalomyelitis (ME). Sometimes it is abbreviated as ME/CFS. The cause of CFS is unknown, although there are many theories, ranging from viral infections to psychological stress.

SOUL HOLES THAT MAY CAUSE CHRONIC FATIGUE SYNDROME: self-hatred, anxiety, performance, loss of identity, "drivenness," false burden bearing, performance to meet the expectations of others, guilt, and shame

A MODEL PRAYER FOR CHRONIC FATIGUE SYNDROME:

Dear Heavenly Father,

I purpose and choose with my free will to repent for self-hatred, anxiety, performance, loss of identity, "drivenness," false burden bearing, performance to meet the expectations of others, guilt, and shame. I ask that You forgive me, and I forgive myself for operating out of these soul holes. I cancel this debt in Jesus' name, and I ask that You heal me of Chronic Fatigue Syndrome. Holy Spirit, please speak Your words of truth.

AFFLICTION—DEGENERATIVE DISC DISEASE

DEFINITION—Osteoarthritis of the spine, usually in the neck or lower back is a condition of the discs between vertebra causing loss of cushioning, fragmentation, and herniation related to aging.

SOUL HOLES THAT MAY CAUSE DEGENERATION DISC DISEASE: unresolved rejection by an earthly father, fear, stress, self-bitterness, depression, addictions, hope deferred, bitterness, and false burden bearing

A MODEL PRAYER FOR DEGENERATIVE DISC DISEASE:

Dear Heavenly Father,

I purpose and choose with my free will to repent for unresolved rejection by my father, fear, stress, self-bitterness, depression, addictions, hope deferred, bitterness, and false burden bearing. Lord, I ask that You forgive me, and I forgive myself for these sins that I have harbored in my soul. I forgive my father for rejecting me and ask You, Lord, to forgive me for rejecting You. I cancel this debt of Degenerative Disc Disease, in Jesus' mighty name.

AFFLICTION—FIBROMYALGIA

DEFINITION—Fibromyalgia is a disorder characterized by widespread musculoskeletal pain accompanied by fatigue, sleep loss, and memory and mood issues. Researchers believe that fibromyalgia amplifies painful sensations by affecting the way your brain processes pain signals.

SOUL HOLES THAT MAY CAUSE FIBROMYALGIA: anxiety, "drivenness," striving, feeling spiritually uncovered, self-hatred, fear, trauma, depression, idolatry, looking to men for security, lack of nurturing or protection by a natural father, husband, or males in general, and extreme stress

A MODEL PRAYER FOR FIBROMYALGIA:

Dear Heavenly Father,

I purpose and choose with my free will to repent of anxiety, "drivenness," striving, self-hatred, fear, trauma, depression, idolatry in looking to men for security, not feeling covered, nurtured, or protected by a natural father, husband, or males in general, and extreme stress. Lord, I ask that You forgive me, and I forgive myself for all ways that I have allowed these negative emotions to dwell in my soul as holes. I cancel this debt of Fibromyalgia, in Jesus' name. Holy Spirit, please fill my soul holes, and make me whole, in Jesus' name.

AFFLICTION—INSOMNIA

DEFINITION—Persistent problems falling asleep and staying asleep. Most cases of insomnia are related to poor sleep habits caused by depression, anxiety, lack of exercise, chronic illness, or certain medications.

SOUL HOLES THAT MAY CAUSE INSOMNIA: fear, anxiety, stress, hope deferred, occultism (anything that we put before God), depression, and lack of trust in God

A MODEL PRAYER FOR INSOMNIA:

Dear Heavenly Father,

I purpose and choose with my free will to repent for fear, anxiety, stress, hope deferred, occultism, depression, lack of trust in God. Lord, I ask You to forgive me, and I forgive myself and all others for hurting me. Lord, forgive me for the ways I have tried to hide while sleeping and for not wanting to deal with my issues at hand. Forgive me, Father, for self-neglect, poor eating habits, and too much caffeine intake. I cancel this debt of insomnia, in

Jesus' name. Holy Spirit, please speak Your words of truth, and set me free from me.

AFFLICTION—MIGRAINES

DEFINITION—A headache of varying intensity, often accompanied by nausea and sensitivity to light and sound. Migraine headaches are sometimes preceded by warning symptoms. Triggers include hormonal changes, certain foods and drinks, stress, and exercise.

SOUL HOLES THAT MAY CAUSE MIGRAINES: self-conflict, fear, anxiety, and stress

A MODEL PRAYER FOR MIGRAINES:

Dear Heavenly Father,

I purpose and choose with my free will to repent for self-conflict, fear, anxiety, and stress. I cancel this debt of Migraines now, in Jesus' name. Lord, I ask that You forgive me, and I forgive myself. I also forgive all others who have caused me pain, in Jesus' name. I also break a generational curse of migraines over my family, in Jesus' name. It is finished! Holy Spirit, please speak Your words of truth, and set me free.

AFFLICTION—<u>TUMORS</u>

DEFINITION—A tumor is a mass of tissue formed by an accumulation of abnormal cells. Normally, the cells in your body age, die, and are replaced by new cells. With cancer and other tumors, something disrupts this cycle. Tumor cells grow even though the body does not need them and, unlike normal cells, they don't die.

SOUL HOLES THAT MAY CAUSE TUMORS—nursing old habits, fear, shocks, regrets, bitterness against self, bitterness against others

A MODEL PRAYER FOR TUMORS:

Dear Heavenly Father,

I purpose and choose with my free will to repent for nursing old habits, fear, shocks, regrets, bitterness against self (benign tumors), bitterness against others (malignant tumors). Lord, I ask You to forgive me, and I forgive myself, in Jesus' name. I cancel this debt of tumors, in Jesus' name. Holy Spirit, please tell me how I gave these tumors a right to come into my body. As I receive Your insight, may I dive deep within my soul and uproot every lie that has caused my soul holes. God, show me how to let go of the old and allow Your glory to fill me with Your wholeness.

183

Over the last twenty-three years, as I have sought God's face, He has granted me a taste of wisdom, understanding, and insight into such matters. The greatness of God is that He created our bodies to heal themselves. Through this understanding of soul holes, we have a greater opportunity to be healed, and our bodies can become whole. We no longer have to fall prey to the tactics of the devil.

There is a reason for everything that God has ever said, but have we really understood what He has said? I will be the first to say that I have not fully understood the words of God. What I do know is that those who seek shall find. Find what? We will find the *truth* that sets us all free. If the promises in the Word of God are true, prosperous, and full of health and wealth, then why are Christians so sick, broke, and disgusted? The truth of God is powerful enough to part a sea, impregnate a virgin, raise the dead, and open blinded eyes, deaf ears, and tombs. The question is not if God can; the question is why can't we?

THE GREATNESS OF GOD IS THAT HE CREATED OUR BODIES TO HEAL THEMSELVES!

If we can't, we need to know that God can. We have an important part to play in our healing. We can't expect God to do everything without us stepping up to the plate. If we can come out of denial, identify our soul holes, repent, and ask God to fill us, then we can get our souls made whole to carry the glory of God.

The issue is not God; the issue is that we haven't dealt with our soul holes. We can hide issues in our souls because no one can see into our souls. Many say that the eyes are the window of one's soul. The trouble is that we aren't looking each other in the eye! Everyone is looking down at their smart phones while participating in false intimacy via electronics. If we are to be the temple of God, we must get our souls swept clean of all unclean spirits that have been housed there. We need our eyes of understanding enlightened:

> *The eyes of your understanding being enlightened;*
> *that ye may know what is the hope of his calling,*
> *and what the riches of the glory of his inheritance*
> *in the saints.*   Ephesians 1:18

This is going to take some work because we have allowed our soul holes to get deeper and wider over time. We have not known how to deal with our undealt-with issues. This lack of knowledge is what has kept us spiritually handi-capped. We haven't let other people help us because we were too ashamed of what was lodged in our souls. The truth is that we all fall short of God's glory. It is time for the Body of Christ to be set free, so that we will be able to live our lives free from the soul holes that have plagued us for generations.

This is the generation that will rise up and take its place, which until now has kept our ancestors from going into the promises here on earth as it is in heaven:

> *Arise, shine; for thy light is come, and the glory of the* Lord *is risen upon thee.*   Isaiah 60:1

Are you ready to experience the fullness of God in a way that you have only heard about from others? Are you ready to be free from your own issues that torment you in the midnight hour? Are you ready to see your children free from the repetitious patterns of destruction? If so, here we go. We are about to travel into the greatest and most successful land of our lives and conquer things that have never been conquered. Travel to unravel.

1. IDENTIFY SOUL HOLES
2. COME OUT OF DENIAL OF UNDEALT-WITH ISSUES AND EMOTIONS
3. HUMBLE YOURSELF, REPENT, AND ASK THE LORD TO FILL YOU WITH HIS GLORY

On page 184 is a model prayer, followed in the next page by a list of common soul holes that I wanted to share with you. I have seen diseases cured, blinded eyes and deaf ears opened, cancers healed, and souls saved with this one little twenty-second prayer. Pray the prayer, filling in the blanks with the soul hole or holes that best describe what you have experienced. Never despise your small beginnings:

For who hath despised the day of small things? for they shall rejoice, and shall see the plummet in the hand of Zerubbabel with those seven; they are the eyes of the Lord, which run to and fro through the whole earth. Zechariah 4:10

Always remember, little is much when God is in it! Please visit our website for a free copy of the Soul Hole Prayer and the list of soul holes, so that you can share them with others.

SOUL HOLE PRAYER

Dear Heavenly Father,

I purpose and choose with my free will to repent of allowing the soul hole of _____
to reside in my heart as sin. Lord, I ask You to forgive me, and I forgive myself for any way that I have nurtured and protected this hole in my soul. I forgive all others for causing me pain and cancel this debt of
_____ now, in Jesus' name.
Holy Spirit, please heal my soul holes and speak Your words of truth. Amen!

After praying, always take the time to be still and listen to what the Holy Spirit desires to say to you.

—Examples of Soul Holes—

Abandonment	Self-Abandonment	Performance	Abandonment from Father
Accusation	Slander	Regret	Abandonment from Mother
Scorn	Addiction	Drunkenness	Food Addictions
Anger	Hatefulness	Hostility	Repressed Anger
Anxiety	Worry	Drivenness	Self-Bitterness
Bitterness	Grief	Inherited Confusion	Drug Dependence
Confusion	Harshness	Memory Loss	Stuffed Bitterness
Ridicule	Envy/Jealousy	Slander	Critical/Judgmental
Deception	Lying	Manipulation	Need To Be Loved
Doubt/Unbelief	Rebellion	Double-mindedness	Lack of Discernment
Dumb and Deaf	Unresolved Conflicts	Occult	Lack of Trust in God
Self-Neglect	Impatience	Rage	False Burden Bearing
Fear	Fear of Man	Fear of Death	Fear of Pain
Hatred	Self-Hatred	Self-Destruction	Stuffed anger
Hope Deferred	Guilt	Shame	Self-Conflict
Insecurity	Mistrust	Cynicism	Need to Dominate
Perversion	Rejection	Self-Rejection	Trauma from Sexual Abuse
Pornography	Uncleanliness	Sexual Sin	Rejection From Father
Fornication	Homosexuality	Adultery	Rejection From Mother
Stress	Pessimism	Perfectionism	Trauma
Pain	Discouragement	Fear of the Future	Hardness of Heart
Heaviness	Broken Heart	Torment	Oppression/Depression
Panic Attacks	Schizophrenia	Social Isolation	Insanity
Pity	Self-Pity	Nursing Old Hurts	Living in the Past
Pride	False Humility	Resentment	Arrogance
Unforgiveness	Victimization	Overly Sensitive	Lost Identity

These are just a few examples of soul holes that you can start *"praying around with."* Don't forget to get your free copies of the Soul Hole Prayer and the list of Soul Holes to give to your loved ones as a gift to help them get their soul holes healed. Reading this whole book would also be beneficial to them.

CHAPTER 7

FREE INDEED

If the Son therefore shall make you free, ye shall be free indeed.   John 8:36

Whom the Son sets free is free indeed. Are you ready to be free?

I love this passage of scripture. God's desire is that His children be set free from any and all of the things that bring dis-ease to their souls. As you walk in this newfound life of freedom, you will become more and more free to be who God called you to be. We have walked in the shoes of our ancestors for too long; it's time for us to be "foot loose and fancy free."

There is always more to be experienced, so we must not settle for less than God's best:

Because the creature itself also shall be delivered from the bondage of corruption into the glorious liberty of the children of God.   Romans 8:21

It's time to be delivered from the bondage of our ancestors and from the things that they taught us by way of tradition. If we are not careful, we can make the Word of God *"of none effect"* because of what our forefathers taught us:

> *Making the word of God of none effect through your tradition, which ye have delivered: and many such like things do ye.* Mark 7:13

I love what God told Moses the day Moses saw the burning bush of God's glory:

> *And he said, Draw not nigh hither: put off thy shoes from off thy feet, for the place whereon thou standest is holy ground.* Exodus 3:5

In other words, take off the shoes of tradition. This place would be unlike any other place where mankind had ever walked before. God had Moses to take of his shoes so that nothing would cover the soles of his feet. God wants us to take off everything that has artificially covered our walk with Him.

After Moses got his shoes off, God used him to set an entire nation free. Learn how to walk in God's footsteps and not in the traditions of men, and you will always see the glory of the Lord.

God sent His only begotten son to die on the cross for our sins and to save us from eternal torment:

For God so loved the world, that he gave his only be-gotten Son, that whosoever believeth in him should not perish, but have everlasting life.   John 3:16

Many people get saved, but then they stop there. Salvation is the greatest message that I preach for the Kingdom of God, but salvation is not just a one-time event, like most people believe. Deciding to accept Jesus Christ as your Lord and Savior will be the greatest decision you will ever make. It is like the act of taking off your shoes to begin walking out your salvation. But once your soul is saved, don't stop there. Seek more of God.

If you are reading this book and you have never accepted Jesus as your Lord and Savior, or if you have walked away from God, I would love to have the opportunity just now to lead you in a prayer:

Dear Heavenly Father,

I come to You, acknowledging that I am a sinner, and I need Your forgiveness to set me free from all of my sins. I ask that You forgive me, and I forgive myself and all others. I ask You to come into my heart and save my soul, in Jesus' name. Lord, set me free from me, that I may be all that You have chosen me to be.

Amen!

When I first invited Jesus into my heart and started going to church, I wondered why people wanted to hurry up and get out of church. It bothered me that people became anxious around noon and were ready to leave the Sunday morning service. I decided to stay at church after everyone else had left. I would sit there and ask God to tell me everything that He wanted to tell those people who wouldn't listen. All God wants is our attention, and if you won't give it to Him, then He will give your blessing to another.

Even now, when I do conferences, I pray that the people will receive all that God has for them. If they don't, then I will receive their portion. You have to hunger and thirst for the glory of God, just as you do with physical hunger and thirst. We should be so hungry for God that we never stop seeking Him, even when it is time to eat lunch. God is looking for the Lion of Judah to roar. Don't be surprised if the roar comes from within your belly first, as you desperately seek Him. Several of the other young people joined me in my search for God, and before long we had a large group of people who were interested in meeting after the traditional service.

We were so hungry for God that He showed up, demonstrating His signs, wonders, and miracles. Before we knew it, people were coming back to church, because the day was nearly over, and it was time for the regular evening service. This went on for several years, and many people were being saved, healed, and delivered because of their hunger, which had been brought forth by the presence of God. We called these our "MORE" services.

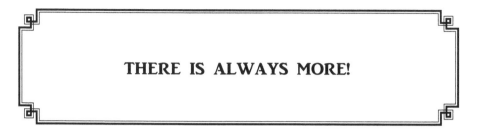

THERE IS ALWAYS MORE!

Last summer, God called me to fast for forty days. I was excited to see and hear all that He was desiring to reveal to me. Space does not allow me to tell everything that He revealed to me while on the forty-day fast, but I can tell you that great and mighty things are taking place in this earth realm because "*the remnant*" is desperate to see God's face. The Lion of Judah is roaring. You must make sure that the roar of your flesh is not louder than the roar of Judah. Whatever you crave most is what you will receive the greatest dose of. If you desire to see great and mighty things, then you must make great and mighty changes.

I'm not saying that you must go on a forty-day fast as I did, but I am saying that if there is no sacrifice, there is no hunger. Desperation is what makes it possible to see MORE of God. Think about some of the most desperate times and darkest days you have experienced in life. It was in those dark, desperate days that you saw the MORE of God. God did not cause your despair, but He was there to bring you through it.

During one of my most desperate times, God allowed me to write *The Forty-Day Soul Fast*.[9] The book consists of forty days of prayerful devotions that help you to get to the place you deserve to be and make it possible for God to use you

---

9. Self-Published 2015

in these days in which we live. *The Forty-Day Soul Fast* will lead you through forty days of fasting the negative emotions that feed your soul holes.

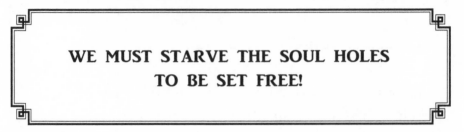

WE MUST STARVE THE SOUL HOLES TO BE SET FREE!

As you continue to work on your soul holes and get free, you will see just how desperate you are. Your despair has brought forth a lot of calamity and confusion to your life. The despair that we go through must be given to God, so He can use it to bring healing to our souls. We get so wrapped up in the situations and circumstances that come our way that we seldom look at despair as an opportunity to see more of God. We have lived with our soul holes for so long that we automatically allow them to dictate our emotions.

This insanity must come to a stop! It is time to get our soul holes healed, so that we can use our time to go deeper into the presence of God. In the presence of God is fullness of joy:

> *Thou wilt shew me the path of life: in thy presence is fulness of joy; at thy right hand there are plea-sures for evermore.* Psalm 16:11

We must trade in our worn-out shoes (souls) of our own will and walk bare before the Lord. It is the joy of the Lord that we need in order to become strong enough to overcome our soul holes. God needs a people to stand as a demonstration of His glory:

> *Then he said unto them, Go your way, eat the fat, and drink the sweet, and send portions unto them for whom nothing is prepared: for this day is holy unto our Lord: neither be ye sorry; for the joy of the Lord is your strength.* Nehemiah 8:10

I was watching my son play a new video game the other day. I don't know a lot about video games, but I like to see how God uses everything in life to teach us more about His glory. The good guy was fighting the bad guys to the end, to ensure that goodness prevailed. Interestingly, the good guy went into a cave to find a certain power so he could move to the next level. In the cave, there was a large enough hole so that he could walk all around in the middle of the cave. Water was falling in the center of the hole, and it looked like a waterfall. The powers the good guy needed to have enough strength to continue his journey were in that water.

Spiritually, I compared the large hole to a soul hole, and the water in the middle of the soul hole represented the truth it took to overcome the evil. We must get to the center of our dehydrated soul holes and apply the truth (water) to any dry place where evil has tried to reside. The good always wins in the end, but our job is to get to the center of the evil and overcome it with the truth of God.

In order to overcome our many soul holes, we must begin to call evil what it is and stop justifying it as being good.

Woe unto them that call evil good, and good evil;
that put darkness for light, and light for darkness;
that put bitter for sweet, and sweet for bitter.

Isaiah 5:20

As you get stronger and stronger in overcoming soul holes that have affected you for years, you will learn how to recognize the difference between the truth and a lie. You will begin to react differently, and things that used to bother you won't even phase you anymore. Things that got on your nerves before suddenly lose their ability to influence you in a negative way. Every time you get a soul hole healed, you will become closer to becoming the genuine person God created you to be.

We have been so full of holes that we really didn't even know who God had created us to be. Have you ever wished you could be happier than you are? Well, you can be, because God created you to be happy.

Have you ever wished you could be more prosperous than you are? It is because God created you to be prosperous. Have you ever wished you had more peace than you have? God created you to have peace. Our soul holes have stolen our joy, our prosperity, and our peace, and there are many more promises that we have yet to receive.

The good thing about God's Word is that we don't have to wish. We are children of the Most High, so we don't have to wish or be lucky in order to walk in the promises of God. All we have to do is hunger and thirst after righteousness:

*Blessed are they which do hunger and thirst after
righteousness: for they shall be filled.* Matthew 5:6

Filled with what? Filled with righteousness! *Righteousness* is "the quality of being morally right." It is "doing what is right," both according to the truth of God and the laws of man. Righteousness is the decision that we make to walk in the truth.

Our soul holes are not formed out of righteousness; they are formed out of painful experiences which form unrighteousness. Therefore, when we react out of our soul holes, we are put in the category of the unrighteous. Righteousness is the truth that sets our souls free, to be all that God has called us to be.

As a matter of fact, everything that we need is already in us; we just have to let it come forth. Our responsibility is to get our soul holes filled with the truth, so that righteousness can come forth. The promises of God have always been within us, but our soul holes have lied to us and wreaked havoc upon us. It is time to arise and shine, for the glory of the Lord has risen upon us:

> *Arise, shine; for thy light is come, and the glory of
> the LORD is risen upon thee.* Isaiah 60:1

THE TEMPLE OF THE LORD

It is time for us to arise out of our slumber, wipe our eyes, stretch, and then get busy kicking some butt. We usually only say BUT when we are trying to justify our unrighteousness.

For example, "I know I have anger issues, BUT I got them honestly." We must stop justifying our soul holes and get them healed, or we will always be the BUTT. We are destined to be the head and not the tail.

We have been asleep far too long, because we have participated in the deceptive ways in which our soul holes have affected us. We are not defeated, insecure, fearful, abandoned, forsaken, misunderstood, rejected, ignorant, confused, impatient, angry, bitter, hateful, rigid, cruel, overly-sensitive, addicted, anxious, critical, perverted, stressed, oppressed, depressed, pitiful, prideful, self-abandoned, drunkards, worried, unresolved, guilt-filled, heavy, schizophrenic, regretful, hostile, grief-stricken, envious, manipulating, occultic, shameful, self-destructive, mistrusting, hard-hearted, resentful, harsh, slanderous, rageful, discouraged, tormented, insane, living in the past, or arrogant victims. We can no longer continue to allow these soul holes to accuse us of being any of these unrighteous things.

God's Word tells me that I was once all of these things, but I have come out of the darkness, to live in the light:

> *And such were some of you: but ye are washed, but ye are sanctified, but ye are justified in the name of the Lord Jesus, and by the Spirit of our God.*
> 1 Corinthians 6:11

God chose us to walk in His truth before the foundation of the world. Are we truth-walkers or word-talkers? Are we a demonstration of the Word or just a presentation of the world? People today no longer want to just hear the Word; they want to see a demonstration of God's Word:

> *But ye are a chosen generation, a royal priesthood, an holy nation, a peculiar people; that ye should shew forth the praises of him who hath called you out of darkness into his marvellous light; Which in time past were not a people, but are now the people of God: which had not obtained mercy, but now have obtained mercy. Dearly beloved, I beseech you as strangers and pilgrims, abstain from fleshly lusts, which war against the soul; having your conversation honest among the Gentiles: that, whereas they speak against you as evildoers, they may by your good works, which they shall behold, glorify God in the day of visitation.* 1 Peter 2:9-12

To live in the light and be a demonstration, we must get our soul holes healed.

The word *demon* spelled backwards is *no-med*. Soul holes eventually demand medication because our sick soul influences our whole body. Medication masks the affliction and pacifies the pain, all the while the soul holes continue to get deeper. When we get our souls healed from afflictions, then we can experience a demonstration of God. He knew that one day a righteous people would arise out of their slumber and become a DEMONSTRATION for the Kingdom of God. Demons must flee in the presence of a godly demonstration.

ARE WE WALKERS OR
JUST TALKERS OF THE TRUTH?

We must come out of the legalistic mind-set that Christians can't have unclean spirits. I will call them unclean spirits because most Christians don't like the word *demon*. Our soul holes are indentions that are left in our souls as a result of painful experiences. Unclean spirits can dwell in these soul holes until they are evicted by the truth.

The truth can't come until we are aware of the need to be set free. As we humble ourselves, allow the truth to come in, and repent, then (and only then) can we be set free. The unclean spirits have the right to reside in our souls because of the evil <u>demon</u>stration they demand. In other words, if you have a soul hole of rejection and experience a situation in which you feel rejected, you may respond by allowing the soul hole of rejection to be <u>demon</u>strated.

A demonstration of a soul hole will disqualify you as being a righteous demonstration for the Lord. The soul hole of rejection may demonstrate itself by saying things like, "I don't care if they like me or not," or "I didn't want to go with them anyway."

The unclean spirit of rejection is able to control your thoughts and actions. The more you allow the unclean spirit to dominate your soul, the more potential it has to overcome you. One may say, "Well, everyone deals with rejection!"

That is exactly right, but DEAL is the key word. You have to deal with that evil...unless you want it to eat your relationships alive or maybe even eat your body alive. When people get hurt by others, have you ever heard them say, "This is eating me alive," or "they make me sick"? Be careful not to allow your soul holes to prophesy your future. Soul holes love to demonstrate.

WHAT ARE YOU DEMONSTRATING?

It was rejection that caused Jesus to be crucified. God's people rejected Jesus. Why is rejection a sin? First of all, it brings death to relationships. Second, it is not good and perfect. And lastly, it damages both your soul and other people. Hurt people hurt other people. The saga remains the same, and no one gets healed of the blame game. What are you demonstrating?

I have never understood why people have been so attracted to daytime dramas. When I was a child, people liked to watch "Days of Our Lives." I just happened to tune into that program the other day, and the story line is just the same as it was forty years ago. The same people are sleeping with the same people outside of marriage. The same business partners are cheating and stealing money from the same firm. The same drunkards are getting in the same head-on collisions and waking up from their comas to find their spouses in the arms of their best friends.

This is America's entertainment. And we wonder why our children turn out the way that they do? We are drawn to what lies within our souls. If you like to be entertained by this kind of drama, guess what lies in your soul? The entertainment world is full of soul-hole demonstrations. Soul holes will be attracted to the same soul holes in others. Why do you think it is so attractive to the world? The same dramas are going on in our souls that go on in the world...that is, if we allow our soul holes to remain.

Hollywood might as well call its industry Inner-retainment. We have been retained by our soul hole drama far too long. Now is the time to arise and shine and be your own star.

> *The star of who you really are, by far,*
> *Is not the scar*
> *That still resides inside,*
> *As it collides with other soul holes,*
> *To delete your goal of being made whole.*
> *Arise and shine, My glory divine,*
> *Come away from the drama of time,*
> *To shine in the darkest places of your soul,*
> *To find that you are the treasure of My gold.*
> *Dust off your soul and be made whole,*
> *To find My glory divine.*
> *It is time to shine.*
> *From sea to shining sea,*
> *It is time for you to be like Me.*

In this hour, we must demonstrate the truth and power that God has given to us to share with others who cannot see. Not everyone sees the truth, but when one seeks God, there is more in store than one can find and explore. All

204

eternity longs to be by our side, in a demonstration, as we overcome our pride.

No longer must we hide what is on the inside. We must come out of hiding and strive to become all and not just some. Let us all deal with what lies to us on the inside, that has caused holes in our soul. May we let the truth of God make us whole. May we allow God to have His way today, so that we may say, "All of You and less of me, come what may."

I just want to be the light that God has called me to be, so that I may see the fruit, the root, and the tree in totality. I don't want to miss what God has for me on earth as it is in heaven. I want completion, as in the number seven. "Complete in me all that You have in store, and allow me to walk through Your open door. Help me to overcome the holes in my soul so that I can be all that You have called me to be."

Identify your soul holes, come out of denial, humble yourself, repent, and be set free. Everything else will work itself out when you begin to operate in this manner. Truth has a way of being "the way." It will either be your way or Yahweh. We have to be careful not to get in the way of our own healing. You will begin to see the truth as it sets you free. You are about to live life to its fullest.

After you identify your soul holes and come out of denial, then repent and get your soul holes filled, you will begin to live the abundant life that Jesus made available for us over two-thousand years ago.

I am confident that we, as Christians, have blamed the devil for a lot of things that our soul holes have caused. I am pretty sure that I am my worst enemy. When we get our soul holes filled, we are going to see a significant difference in the condition of our bodies.

Imagine what it would be like if the Body of Christ would work to get its soul holes filled, what it would be like if the Body of Christ would get healed! The Church was intended to be a type of hospital where sick people could find their healing. Unfortunately, there are more people who are remaining sick than are getting healed. We must see that this insane epidemic of evil soul holes is identified, dealt with, and repented of quickly...before sickness has time to ultimately lead to death.

GET YOUR MONEY HEALED

There is one particular thing that I have noticed in dealing with my soul holes, and it concerns financial healing. My whole life I have struggled financially. As a business owner and platform artist for Loreal, I made a lot of money over the years. But, even though I made a lot of money, I couldn't maintain financial success. Since I have been identifying my soul holes, coming out of denial, humbling myself, and repenting, God has restored my finances, and I am able to manage what He has blessed me with.

As I spoke about earlier in this book, I had to consider my ways:

> *Now therefore thus saith the LORD of hosts; Consider your ways. Ye have sown much, and bring in little; ye eat, but ye have not enough; ye drink, but*

ye are not filled with drink; ye clothe you, but there is none warm; and he that earneth wages earneth wages to put it into a bag with holes. Thus saith the LORD of hosts; Consider your ways.

Haggai. 1:5-7

After I began to consider my ways, the Lord showed me that my soul was like a bag with holes in it. Regardless of how much money I made, I still had those holes. And if you have holes in your money bag, you will lose your money.

If you have holes in your soul, you will lose valuables, such as blessings, relationships, finances, and on and on. I am tired of losing! I am ready to possess and maintain all that God has to pour out on me.

It is important to possess the promises of God, but if you cannot maintain them, then all is in vain. We must rebuild our temples from the ruins of our soul holes and be restored to righteousness for His name's sake:

He restoreth my soul: he leadeth me in the paths of righteousness for His name's sake. Psalm 23:3 [10]

In Haggai 1, the first eleven verses speak of the rebuilding of the temple of the Lord, and verses 12-15 speak of that work being started. In chapter 2, the first nine verses speak of a comparison of the temple, verses 14-19 speak of judgment for uncleanness, and verses 20-23 are subtitled *God's Chosen*

10. I write more about this subject in my pamphlet, **"Possess and Maintain."**

Signet. I love what verses 21 and 22 state:

> *Speak to Zerubbabel, governor of Judah, saying, I will shake the heavens and the earth; and I will overthrow the throne of kingdoms, and I will destroy the strength of the kingdoms of the heathen; and I will overthrow the chariots, and those that ride in them; and the horses and their riders shall come down, everyone by the sword of his brother.*

God loves you so much that He will shake everything in your life that can be shaken, just so that you can get to the truth:

> *For thus saith the LORD of hosts; Yet once, it is a little while, and I will shake the heavens, and the earth, and the sea, and the dry land; and I will shake all nations, and the desire of all nations shall come: and I will fill this house with glory, saith the LORD of hosts. The silver is mine, and the gold is mine, saith the LORD of hosts. The glory of this latter house shall be greater than of the former, saith the LORD of hosts: and in this place will I give peace, saith the Lord of hosts.* Haggai 2:6-9

Soul holes are going to be shaken and awakened in this hour of the demonstration of God's power. This is part of arising and shining, for the glory of the Lord has risen upon you. You will be like a sleeping giant who has suddenly been awakened.

The soul holes that have kept you in slumber have been under the dumb and deaf spirit. Everything that we have is to be shaken by this awakening. Our soul holes have set up a false kingdom in our souls, an evil kingdom that tries to keep us from living a whole life. God must shake us free from the lies that have made us hide from the truth. The foundations of false expectations and the pillars of performance must fall, if we are to have God as our All-in-All. I am ready to trade my soul holes in for a whole soul. How about you?

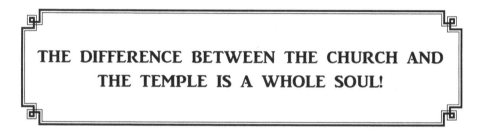

THE DIFFERENCE BETWEEN THE CHURCH AND THE TEMPLE IS A WHOLE SOUL!

The Church tolerates being broken as "just part of life." The Temple is in search for the truth, in order to be set free indeed. The Church is holey, but the Temple is holy.

The whole book of Haggai talks about us becoming a temple for the glory of the Lord to fill. *"For the earth shall be filled with the knowledge of the Lord as the waters cover the sea"* (Haggai 2:14). I am ready to be filled by THE LATTER RAIN of God's glory, so that I may see the Kingdom come on Earth as it is in Heaven. I don't want to be the Church; I want to be the Temple.

The book of Isaiah speaks about this day coming quickly:

> *Then thou shalt see, and flow together, and thine heart shall fear, and be enlarged; because the abun-*

dance of the sea shall be converted unto thee, the forces of the Gentiles shall come unto thee.

Isaiah 60:5

God desires to pour Himself into us as the glory fills the earth (us) and as the waters cover the sea. The abundance of the sea is being converted into thee, and as God's glory is converting us into the sea, we shall see as He sees. We shall become the SEE (SEA).

When we see like God, then the sea can be dismissed:

And I saw a new heaven and a new earth: for the first heaven and the first earth were passed away; and there was no more sea. And I John saw the holy city, new Jerusalem, coming down from God out of heaven, prepared as a bride adorned for her husband. And I heard a great voice out of heaven saying, Behold, the tabernacle of God is with men, and he will dwell with them, and shall be His people, and God himself shall be with them, and be their God. Revelation 21:1-3

In order to be made whole, you must give the Lord your broken spirit that has been crippled by your own condition. After this process of being filled by God's glory, you should be able to contain what God pours into you. After being filled by God's glory, then you will be able to overflow with the promises of eternity out upon a dry and thirsty land. Not only will you be filled; but everywhere you go others will be filled by the presence of God that you contain.

God is not looking for perfection; He is looking for someone to cast a reflection of His glory. We no longer have to live holey; we can live holy. And the saints go marching on!

1. IDENTIFY YOUR SOUL HOLES
2. COME OUT OF DENIAL OF UNDEALT-WITH ISSUES AND EMOTIONS
3. HUMBLE YOURSELF, REPENT, AND ASK THE LORD TO FILL YOU WITH HIS GLORY

"Mine eyes have seen the glory of the coming of the Lord;

He is trampling out the vintage Where the grapes of wrath are stored;

He hath loosed the fateful Lightening of His terrible swift sword:

His truth goes marching on.

Glory, glory, hallelujah!

Glory, glory, hallelujah!

Glory, glory, hallelujah!

His truth goes marching on.

I have seen Him in the watch-fires of a hundred circling camps,

They have builded Him an altar in the evening dews and damps;

I can read His righteous sentence by the dim and flaring lamps;

His truth goes marching on.
Glory, glory, hallelujah!
Glory, glory, hallelujah!
Glory, glory, hallelujah!
His truth goes marching on.

I have read a fiery gospel writ in burnished rows
of steel:
As ye deal with my contemners so with you my
grace shall deal;
Let the Hero, born of woman, crush the serpent with
his heel,
Since God is marching on.

He has sounded forth the trumpet that shall never
call retreat;
He is sifting out the hearts of men before His judg-
ment-seat;
Oh, be swift, my soul, to answer Him! Be jubilant,
me feet!
Our God is marching on.
Glory, glory, hallelujah!
Glory, glory, hallelujah!
Glory, glory, hallelujah!
His truth goes marching on.

In the beauty of the lilies Christ was born across
the sea,

With a glory in His bosom that transfigures you and me.
As He died to make men holy, let us die to make men free,
While God is marching on.
Glory, glory, hallelujah!
Glory, glory, hallelujah!
Glory, glory, hallelujah!
His truth goes marching on.   —Julia Ward Howe
COME ON, SAINTS, LET'S GO MARCHING ON

THE END

AUTHOR CONTACT

You may contact the author, Rebecca L. King, in the following ways:

Website: www.rkingministries.com
email: info@rkingministries.com

Rebecca King Ministry Resources

The Well of God's Glory Unveiled will take you from your living room into the story of one woman's experience at an old family well, where ancient mysteries were unveiled, and generational curses were broken in the glory of God!

Quotes Birthed Out of the Revelation of God's Glory is not your typical literary companion. Filled with enigmatic proverbs given straight from the Throne, this book will move you out of the place of desolation and into the place of revelation!

As the second volume of Quotes Birthed Out of the Revelation of God's Glory, this book is the epitome of the language of Heaven. In addition to the enigmatic proverbs, each section is concluded with a prayer to take you from the desert to the garden!

Interested in walking in the supernatural realm of God's glory? Check out Portals of Heaven for insights on how you, too, can be free from brokenness and finally have the opportunity to experience eternity invading the Earth realm!

The **Portals of Heaven Package** is a dynamic duo teaching on the simplicity and importance of the supernatural realm. With the book and 3-CD set combined, you are guaranteed to receive revelation and insights on how accessible it is to access eternity here on Earth!

The **Glory & Intimacy Manual** is the product of a three-day event where true intimacy is the center of attention. This manual is perfect for Bible study groups who are interested in learning about the glory of God, His true intimacy, and how to search out the depths of the supernatural!

Birthed during a nine-month trial, the **40 Day Soul Fast** book is anything but a normal devotional. Instead of denying yourself food, this "soul fast" teaches you how to rid yourself of the negative emotions we all face on a daily basis.

The **Portals of Heaven** 3-disc set is a perfect addition to the Portals of Heaven book. Filled with even more revelation concerning the supernatural realm of eternity, this is exactly what you need to finish your study of heavenly portals.

From Victim to Victor is a powerhouse teaching that follows the enticing story of how one servant's victimization turns into a glorious victory. Full of scriptural references, life-changing prayers, and relatable stories, you can expect to receive healing and wholeness as you apply the revelation in this teaching. Victory can be yours today. Are you ready?

The Turning Your Ugly into His Glory teaching has the potential to take your ashes of brokenness and turn them into His glorious beauty. Have you had a hard time getting over the "ugly" in your life? Many times we suppress our ugly, and it affects not only us, but others as well. Are you ready to evict your evil and walk in the freedom your heart has desired? If so, take the plunge

It is easy for us to become wrapped up in the confusions of our daily lives. This powerful booklet, **Turning Your Clouds of Confusion into Clouds of His Glory,** will take that confusion and break it down to show you what your destiny truly is: to walk in God's glory!

The Spirit of Elijah CD teaches on Elijah's journey from Gilgal to the Jordan. The glory of God transported Elijah to his rightful, eternal position to fulfill his earthly assignment. Will you allow God to take you from the point of contact to the entrance of Heaven's gateway, to become the fragrance to flow down to others?

Rebecca King Ministries
108 W. Washington Ave.
Nashville, GA 31639
www.rkingministries.com

For questions about our products or booking events, call 229-646-7009 or
email us at info@rkingministries.com